AF600506

DOUBT IN CANON LAW
A HISTORICAL SYNOPSIS AND A COMMENTARY

THE CATHOLIC UNIVERSITY OF AMERICA
CANON LAW STUDIES
No. 346

DOUBT IN CANON LAW

A HISTORICAL SYNOPSIS AND A COMMENTARY

A DISSERTATION

Submitted to the Faculty of the School of Canon Law of the Catholic University of America in Partial Fulfillment of the Requirements for the Degree of Doctor of Canon Law

BY

ROGER VIAU, S.T.L., J.C.L.
Priest of the Diocese of Springfield, Massachusetts

THE CATHOLIC UNIVERSITY OF AMERICA PRESS
WASHINGTON, D. C.
1954

Nihil Obstat:

EDWARD G. ROELKER, S.T.D., J.C.D.,
Censor Deputatus.

Washington, D. C., June 17, 1953.

Imprimatur:

✠ CHRISTOPHER J. WELDON, D.D.,
Bishop of Springfield.

Springfield, Massachusetts, June 23, 1953.

THE WICKERSHAM PRINTING CO.
Lancaster, Penna.

FOREWORD

Doubt has ever been somewhat of a problem in human affairs. Whether it proceed from inadequacy of expression or from lack of perspicacity in the realm of ideas, man is continually harassed in his communion with his fellowmen by a certain amount of misinterpretation. While such a situation is readily understandable in the light of the human condition, in certain domains it becomes an inconvenience. Such an area is the field of legislation. Because law plays such a fundamental rôle in man's life, doubt concerning law begets significant indecision.

The purpose of this dissertation is to present a historical synopsis and a canonical commentary on the positive enactment which the Church has made relative to doubt involved in the interpretation of its own legislation. It can be said that Canon 15 is a juridical innovation. This must not be understood to mean that the problem of doubt in law was ignored before the advent of the Code of Canon Law. On the contrary, the *Corpus Iuris Canonici* contains numerous solutions of dubious matters, but the legislator had not yet presented a positive rule to which an individual could advert in order to solve his doubts. The elaboration of a clear legislative determination was a slow process. It came to fruition after great strides had been made in theology and in the philosophy of law. This development, then, will form the core of the historical section, after which the present legislation will be analyzed.

The writer wishes to express his gratitude to His Excellency the Most Reverend Christopher J. Weldon, D.D., Bishop of Springfield, for the opportunity to pursue advanced studies in Canon Law and for his kind generosity in making this publication possible. He is also indebted to the members of the Faculty of the School of Canon Law for their encouragement and scholarly direction throughout his stay at the Catholic University of America.

TABLE OF CONTENTS

CHAPTER V

CHAPTER VI

CHAPTER I

THE CONCEPT OF DOUBT

Doubt is nowhere defined in the Code of Canon Law. Nonetheless, it is imperative that one have a true notion of doubt, in order to appraise correctly the legal areas in which it plays a definite rôle. For the achievement of this purpose, doubt will first be considered in its intimate nature and, subsequently, there will be analyzed various species of doubt.

Roman Law understood doubt as a word synonymous with uncertainty, ambiguity, obscurity; in short, a doubt existed whenever clarity was lacking or interpretation was needed for the understanding of a law.[1] The *Corpus Iuris Canonici*, while it never formally studied the concept of doubt, accepted the term very much in the same sense as did the Roman jurists. Doubt is contrasted against certitude and clarity.[2]

Article 1. The Nature of Doubt

The philosophers were the first to examine doubt in its proper perspective, because doubt, of its very nature, pertains to the realm of rational psychology. It is primarily a state of the mind with respect to adherence to truth. Whether this truth be of the legal or the moral order, the fundamental analysis concerning the nature of doubt must be derived from psychology. The juridical and the moral fields will of necessity accept the conclusions of philosophy and apply them to their respective fields.

St. Thomas Aquinas (1225-1274), in his *De Veritate*, set forth a thorough investigation of the various states of the mind when it is face to face with the two aspects of a contradiction. In

[1] D. (L, 17) 56, 67, 96, 114; D. (XXXIV, 5) 12, 21, 26.

[2] C. 9, D. II; c. 7, D. XXXIII; c. 3, D. XXV; c. 74, C. II, q. 3; c. 16, D. I, *de cons.*; *glossa* in c. 16, X, *de testibus*, II, 20; c. 3, X, *de sponsalibus et matrimoniis*, IV, 1; c. 12, X, *de homicidio*, V, 12; c. 5, X, *de sententia excommunicationis*, V, 39; c. 25, X, *de verborum significatione*, V, 40; c. 2, X, *de regulis iuris*, V, 41; etc.

order to estimate the comparative adherence of the intellect to truth, he drew up a scale whose gamut ran from doubt to faith. Indeed, the human mind can react quite diversely to the alternatives of a contradiction. At times, it is not more strongly drawn to one than it is to the other. Such a situation results either from the lack of evidence, or it may derive from the apparent counterbalancing weight of the motivating causes which fairly equally draw the intellect to either alternative. Thus philosophy describes doubt and goes on to define it as the fluctuation of the mind between the two alternatives of a contradiction.[3]

Doubt, consequently, is that state of the mind wherein one withholds assent to either alternative of a contradiction. The intellect finds itself unable to anchor itself to truth, not because of some subjective impediment, nor because it fails to grasp the wording of the contradiction. On the contrary, the contradiction either sheds no light or only such light as will not permit the acceptance of one aspect of the contradiction and the rejection of the other. As a result, the mind is not moved to prefer one alternative over the other.

The philosophical exposition of the nature of doubt, as elucidated by St. Thomas, has been widely accepted. However, in the course of the centuries, the concept has been broadened to include opinion. Opinion has also been described by the Angelic Doctor. At times, he stated, the human mind is drawn more strongly to one aspect of a contradiction than it is to the other. Nonetheless, this inclination does not so completely engage the intellect that it is totally determined to that one alternative. It accepts the one aspect, but it always has doubts relative to the other. Hence, opinion is defined as the acceptance of one alternative of a contradiction with some fear regarding the other.[4]

[3] St. Thomas Aquinas, *Quaestiones Disputatae*, I, *De Veritate* (cura et studio P. Fr. Raymundi Spiazzi, O.P., 8. ed. revisa, Taurini-Romae: Marietti, 1949), q. 14, a. 1. This work will henceforth be cited as *De Verit.*

[4] "Quandoque vero intellectus inclinatur magis ad unum quam ad alterum; sed tamen illud inclinans non sufficienter movet intellectum ad hoc quod determinet ipsum in unam partem totaliter; unde accipit quidem unam partem, tamen semper dubitat de opposita. Et haec est dispositio opinantis, qui accipit unam partem contradictionis cum formidine alterius." *De Verit.*, q. 14, a. 1.

It is a state of mind characterized by limited adherence. Opinion, then, differs from doubt only by reason of qualified assent.

It is noteworthy that St. Thomas injected the words " *semper dubitat* " when treating of opinion. Damen, however, in his analysis of this passage, asserts that the word is here employed by the Saint in a broad sense to mean fear.[5] Nonetheless, St. Thomas often used the term in a generic sense without any impropriety. Indeed, doubt can be understood in a twofold proper signification: one, to indicate the state of mind, the other, to mean the objective matter which is not clear and evident, and, hence, engenders doubt in the mind. With respect to the first sense, doubt is distinguished against knowledge (the *scientia* of the Scholastics), in the second it is opposed to certitude, premised on the evidence or the clarity of a matter, so that doubt is considered the equivalent of uncertainty which can be greater or lesser.

When, during the course of the sixteenth and seventeenth centuries, the great controversies raged concerning the various systems of morality, while mention was constantly being made of the philosophical meaning of doubt and of its clear distinction from opinion, the notions of doubt and opinion were effectively considered to be synonymous.[6] While the writer has not encountered any explanation which clearly establishes the acceptance of doubt and opinion as being synonymous, it is most probable that the very text of St. Thomas played a major rôle in determining the intertwining of doubt and opinion. Indeed, if opinion is the mind's qualified acceptance of an alternative, but with a constant doubt as regards the other proposition, there is not and there cannot be possible any kind of certitude. The most that can be attached to opinion is probability. As such, it is not and cannot be a properly prudential basis for legal or moral activity.

5 " Dubitat, dubio scil. lato seu formidine."—" De vitanda iuris correctione ad normam Codicis," *Apollinaris*, V (1932), p. 58, note 11.

6 " Opinio denotat cognitionem dubiam aut probabilem alicujus veritatis." —St. Alphonsus de Ligorio, *Theologia Moralis* (ed. Gaudé, 4 vols., Romae: Typographia Vaticana, 1905-1912), Liber I, n. 59. See also Suarez, *Opera Omnia*, (26 vols., Parisiis: L. Vivès, 1856-1866), Vol. IV, Tractatus *De Bonitate et Malitia Actuum Humanorum*, Disp. XII, sect. II, nn. 6 and 7.

Hence, while the theologians and canonists readily accept these speculative considerations (so many quote this precise article of the *De Veritate*), yet they are also fully aware of the practical difficulties of evaluating the alternatives of a question. They realize that men, as a rule, do not long withhold assent; rather, in the course of ordinary human conduct, the mind, although fearful of error, will espouse one view, exclude the other, and from a position of doubt pass into one of opinion. This explains why Suarez (1548-1617) and St. Alphonsus (1696-1787) maintained that positive doubt nearly always coincides with probable opinion.[7]

As a result of this brief conspectus, one may safely assume that the word "doubt" can be legitimately understood in the generic sense. This signification embraces opinion, and is the usual and proper sense accepted by the moralists and canonists in questions relating to doubt. Hence, it cannot be alleged that such a usage is a contravention of canon 18, which requires that doctrinal interpretation be arrived at according to the proper signification of the terms.

In the Code of Canon Law, doubt is taken to mean a state of the mind in which, because of a positive and objective probability, one gives assent to a view with some fear of falling into error. Thus, according to Michiels, it can be taken to signify all uncertainty arising from any reasonable cause, or based on any positive and objective motive, so that it can truly be probable or reasonably acceptable to a prudent man.[8]

Article 2. The Species of Doubt

Doubt, however well its intimate nature be studied, can be adequately known only if dissected into its component species. Theologians and canonists have endeavored since the medieval period to arrive at the complete division of the subject, and have succeeded with signal success. This article does not propose to

[7] Suarez, *De Bonitate et Malitia Actuum Humanorum,* Disp. XII, sect. II, nn. 6 and 7; St. Alphonsus, *Theologia Moralis,* Liber I, nn. 20 and 59.

[8] G. Michiels, *Normae Generales Iuris Canonici* (2. ed., 2 vols., Parisiis-Tornaci-Romae: Desclée et Socii, 1949), Tom. I, p. 416 (henceforth cited *Normae Generales*).

explore or even to present in its entirety the sum total of their efforts; rather, it will limit its discussion to the scope of the specific types of doubt which play a determining rôle in the canon under consideration.

Doubt can be positive or negative. In this particular instance, doubt is envisaged from the aspect of motive. Doubt is negative when the mind is practically bereft of reasons to support either of two contradictory propositions. It is positive when motives for doubting are present. Thus, positive doubt implies fairly equal reasons for affirming and for denying assent to either proposition, or, as St. Thomas remarked: "There is an apparent equality of motives moving the mind to either consideration."[9] In such a situation, the mind is incapable of forming a judgment, as the motives more or less mutually destroy their respective persuasive force. Negative doubt has been likened to ignorance. Viewed practically, this is true, because in the order of prudence neither can safely be employed. However, the two states should not be theoretically confused, inasmuch as ignorance suggests that the question has not been considered by the mind, whereas negative doubt rather implies that an attempt at evaluation, however inept, has been made, and that such a deliberation did not succeed in arriving at serious motives.

If envisaged from the point of view of the subject, doubt can be objective or subjective. It is objective when in law or in fact there is really present something to respond to the doubt existing in the mind. In a word, a doubt is objective if the positive motives which are proposed are such that they appear based on reality. Doubt is subjective when it exists in the mind alone, without a corresponding basis in reality or in the nature of things. Subjective doubt, then, springs from the lack of proper knowledge or from error. Hence, objective doubt necessarily implies familiarity with the subject at hand.

Law can easily engender some type of doubt; consequently, it will often be necessary to utilize some interpretation to clarify its contents. If a doubt can be dispelled with the use of the

[9] "Quandoque (intellectus) non inclinatur magis ad unum quam ad aliud ...propter apparentem aequalitatem eorum quae movent ad utramque partem." *De Verit.*, q. 14, a. 1.

ordinary interpretative rules or of some particular juridical enactments supplied by the legislator, it is vincible doubt. Occasionally, even after a diligent examination and the application of the legal provisions, it will be impossible to solve a doubt: it is then called an invincible doubt. However, the diligence required in this matter need not be extraordinary; nonetheless, it should closely approximate the care and attention which prudent men ordinarily manifest in important affairs.

Doubt, if viewed in the light of its object, may be distinguished in doubt of law and doubt of fact. A doubt of law is concerned with the law itself and its primary effect, the obligation. Indeed, it arises when, after diligent study, a solution cannot be found relative to the meaning, the extent, the existence, or the cessation of a law. In a wider sense, it may stem from an obligation which derives from a source other than law understood in the strict sense: such would be the case of a precept, a vow or a contract. Hence, a doubt of law can be brought to bear on law alone or on whatever bears the characteristics of an obligation in a particular instance, and on its fundamental elements. The following are offered as examples of a doubt of law: if I doubt that the law commands or forbids something; if I am in doubt as to the existence of a law, or as to its abrogation, or its cessation; if I doubt that a custom has supplanted the law, or that a privilege has modified a law.

Doubt of fact, on the other hand, originates with regard to some particular fact. In such an occurrence, the doubt does not bear on the law itself with clearly exists; rather, it is centered on the fact itself. A fact may be doubtful under two distinct aspects. Indeed, the doubt may arise as to the existence or nonexistence of a fact, such as is the case when there is doubt concerning the valid baptism of a definite person; or else it may question the comprehension of an existing fact under a given law.

These various species of doubt will play a vital rôle in determining the meaning of canon 15, and in circumscribing the respective areas of the Code in which it serves to discover the extent of an obligation attending ecclesiastical laws.

PART I

HISTORICAL SYNOPSIS

CHAPTER II

DOUBT IN THE *CORPUS IURIS CANONICI*

THE question of doubt in law is nowhere formally treated in the *Corpus Iuris Canonici*. The concept of law, while it is discussed in the *Decretum* and in the Decretals, is not fully elaborated. The theologians, and principally St. Thomas Aquinas, in his *Summa Theologiae*, crystallized the doctrine.[1] Hence, it cannot be too surprising if, in turn, doubt in law is sketchily envisaged by the jurists.

It is not the writer's purpose to offer here the complete evolution of the matter from the *Decree of Gratian* to the *Extravagantes*. Rather, the *Corpus Iuris Canonici* will be considered as a juridical entity, and a serious attempt will be made to derive therefrom a synthesis of its solutions and conclusions relative to doubt in law. It would be quite illusory to search through this huge collection in order to seek out a ready-made study of doubt in law: the question was simply not envisaged in this light by the medieval canonists. However true this may be, it must not be construed in such a wise that the legislators and jurists were not interested in this vital problem. On the contrary, they brought to light various principles which proved to be immensely valuable to the theologians in the elaboration of their doctrine concerning the solution of doubts.

[1] *Opera Omnia* (jussu impensaque Leonis XIII, Pontificis Maximi, edita, Romae: Typographia Polyglotta Sacrae Congregationis de Propaganda Fide, 1882-19—), *Summae Theologiae*, Vols. IV-XI (1889-1903), Ia IIae, quaestiones 90-108.

In order to appraise properly the doctrine under study here, it may prove helpful to consider successively tutiorism and the departures from tutioristic principles in the *Corpus Iuris Canonici.*

Article 1. Tutiorism in the *Corpus Iuris Canonici*

A cursory examination of the *Corpus Iuris Canonici* could seem to indicate that tutiorism was the general rule which was invoked for the resolving of doubts in law. While it is true that one could adduce numerous texts to sustain such a contention, it is the purpose of the present article to endeavor to show that tutiorism obtains only in the face of practical doubt and doubt of fact.

In advancing this statement, the writer does not wish to antedate a distinction whose origin lies in the early sixteenth century, and which was propounded for the first time by Cardinal Cajetan (1469-1534), the great commentator of St. Thomas Aquinas. This is simply an attempt to explain in the now accepted form the doctrine which is so often found both in the *Decretum* and in the Decretals. Doubt, by reason of its object, can be either speculative or practical. Both are basically concerned with honesty, but in diverse manners. Speculative doubt strives to seek out the objective morality of an act in the abstract, whereas practical doubt considers the morality of an action to be performed here and now. It is intimately connected with the act itself, while speculative doubt will remain sheer speculation.[2]

A practical doubt may arise from one of two factors: either the law is not clear, or the individual when face to face with the law fails to see its application in a given case. The matters in which practical doubt is most often encountered are danger for one's salvation, danger arising out of an action which must be placed here and now, and, in given instances, the domain of penal law.

It has been the constant teaching of the Church and of the theologians that it is unlawful to act when one is in doubt as to the morality of the action to be performed here and now. For, in so doing, the will entertains a double object here and now

[2] G. Waffelaert, *De dubio solvendo in re morali* (Lovanii, 1880), p. 142.

doubtfully licit. Indeed, this action may be good and it may be evil; and the will, in desiring this double object, must of necessity embrace the evil element, which contains at least the peril of sin. Consequently the will has inclined to sin, and has in effect sinned, because the formal element which colors the morality of the matter at hand is the *periculum peccati* to which one must not expose oneself.

As will be later ascertained, there is contained in the *Corpus Iuris Canonici* a mixture of the internal and the external forums, that is, the legislator will readily solve problems pertaining to the conscience, as well as those which hold sway for the public life of church members. Only too often, the answers do not include the speculative and jurisprudential principles of the doctrine; nonetheless, it is at times possible to discover through a succession of responses to allied topics, the mind of the Church on the issues at stake.

It is in the field of danger for one's salvation that the tutioristic practice of the popes is most easily verified. The security of the individual in regard to his immortal soul stands as a cardinal tenet, and never is one permitted to lose sight of this fact. Evidently, this situation has misled some in their assumption that ecclesiastical authorities at that time were unduly harsh. However, in the absence of a well elaborated juridical science, it is not too surprising to find this timidity on the part of the ones striking out for new solutions: this would eventually be dispelled by the developments in the moral field.

Gratian (+ ca. 1157) incorporated in his *Decretum* (ca. 1140) two texts derived from St. Augustine. They are highly indicative of the mentality prevalent at the time. Both deal with the necessity of a good Christian life, in order that one may feel reasonably secure of obtaining God's mercy. "Do you wish to be freed from doubt? Do you wish to escape uncertainty? Do penance the while you are well."[3] Or again, "Hold to what is certain, and forsake the uncertain."[4]

[3] "Vis ergo a dubio liberari? vis quod incertum est evadere? Age poenitentiam dum sanus es."—C. 2, D. VII, *de poenit.* (Ex Augustino, Liber L Homiliarum, Homilia 41).

[4] "Ergo tene certum, et dimitte incertum."—C. 4, D. VII, *de poenit.* (Ex Augustino, Liber L Homiliarum, Homilia 41).

The gloss found at canon 7, Distinction XXXIII, of the *Decretum* aptly distinguished doubt. The commentator stated that there exists a triple ambiguity: one of law, one of fact and one of person.[5] While no definition of the terms was given, it appears likely that ambiguity of law meant a law which was not clear, and hence was conducive to doubt. Ambiguity of fact encompassed situations in which, while the law was clear, there remained a doubt as to whether a fact existed or fell under the law. Ambiguity of person signified uncertainty as to the real identity of a person, although both the law and the fact in its relation to the law were clear.

The problem of legal ambiguity was summarily dealt with inasmuch as it was identified with the *lacuna legis*. It had nothing to do with the topic of the present study. However, with reference to the ambiguity of fact, the glossator extended himself and set forth basic principles of great value for the matter here under consideration. The first principle held that, in the case of doubt of fact, sentence was never to be meted out to the detriment of anyone: this will be envisaged in a later article.

Yet, it could at times occur that no detriment was visited upon anyone, even if a certain judgment was rendered in a dubious matter. This was especially the case in doubts relative to baptism, ordination and the consecration of churches. In these instances, certainly no harm was suffered by those who were rebaptized or reordained, or by a church which already had been consecrated. The glossator here offered three texts, which each in turn dealt with various phases of this doubt.

The second *capitulum* of Distinction LXVIII presented the response of Pope Gregory I to John, Bishop of Ravenna, on the question of a doubt concerning the true episcopal character of bishops who had ordained some priests. Gregory answered that, if the men so ordained were worthy and fit subjects for the priesthood, they were to receive anew the sacerdotal unction from their own bishops, and then to perform the sacred ministry. Adding his particular comment to this, Gratian stated that,

5 "Sed dicitur quod triplex est ambiguitas: ambiguitas iuris, ambiguitas facti, ambiguitas personae."—*Glossa* ad v. "*ambiguis.*"

while it was forbidden for one who was validly ordained to seek reordination, this was not true of one who had been raised to Orders by a doubtful minister. He proceeded to liken the case to that of a person doubtfully baptized. Such a person was to receive baptism, and, by analogy, the doubtfully ordained were to receive ordination with certainty before assuming the functions of the priesthood. It is not a matter of the reiteration of a sacrament, because if the first ordination was valid, the second produced no effect; on the other hand, if the first was void, the second really made one a priest.[6] In commenting on this text, the glossator stated that in a matter of doubt one was preferably to be considered as not ordained and as not baptized. If such a presumption of law was valid for these sacraments, why did it not equally hold true for matrimony? The other sacraments could be iterated without danger, but in the case of marriage it would be dangerous, especially if it were determined that a marriage did not exist, when in reality it did.[7]

[6] "Presbyteri, quos reperisti, si incogniti fuerint viri illi, qui ordinantur, et dubium est, eos episcopos fuisse, an non, qui eos ordinaverunt, si bonae actionis virique catholici sunt ipsi presbyteri, et in ministerio Christi omnique sancta lege edocti, ab episcopo suo benedictionem presbyteratus suscipiant et consecrentur, et sic ministerio sacro fungantur."—C. 2, D. LXVIII; P. Jaffé, *Regesta Pontificum Romanorum ab condita Ecclesia ad annum post Christum natum* MCXCVIII, (ed. 2 correctam et auctam auspiciis Guglielmi Wattenbach curaverunt F. Kaltenbrunner, P. Ewald, S. Loewenfeld, 2 vols., Lipsiae, 1885-1888), n. 1198.

"Dictum Gratiani: Quod ergo consecratus in eodem ordine iterum consecrari prohibetur, de eo intelligendum est, qui consecratus est ab illo, quem certum erat ius consecrandi habere. Qui autem ab illo consecratur, quem non constat ius consecrandi habuisse, iterum consecrandus est, quia si ille ius consecrandi non habuerit, ille ex olei effusione nihil consecrationis accepit . . ."—Ad c. 2, D. LXVIII.

[7] Hic in dubio potius praesumitur non ordinatus quam ordinatus. Similiter in dubio praesumitur potius non baptizatus quam baptizatus . . . Et in dubio potius praesumitur ecclesia non consecrata quam consecrata . . . Sed cum ita praesumitur in his sacramentis, quare in sacramento matrimonii potius praesumitur pro ipso quam contra ipsum . . . Respondetur: sine omni periculo est si sacramenta illa iterentur. Sed periculosum esset, si iudicaretur non esse matrimonium ubi est.—*Glossa* ad v. *Consecrentur*, c. 2, D. LXVIII.

The same doctrine obtained in respect of the consecration of churches. If a doubt arose inasmuch as the necessary documents or reliable witnesses to establish the certainty of the consecration were lacking, then the church should benefit from a new consecration.[8] This solution was attributed to Pope Felix III, who reigned between 526-530.[9]

Gregory II, writing to Bishop Boniface in the year 726, asserted the necessity, as commanded by reason, of baptizing children who had been taken away from their parents, when it was not known if indeed they had ever received baptism.[10] The *Glossa* quickly added that in such circumstances that which proved the more tenable was to be maintained.[11]

The conclusion to be derived from these texts which dealt with the validity of the sacraments is this: one had to follow the safer course in order not to imperil the eternal salvation of souls. The responses of the pontiffs manifested an early and painstaking solicitude on the part of the Church authorities to leave nothing to chance in this domain. This ancient practice still animates the theology of the sacraments, concerned as it is with man's immortal soul and the necessity of saving it.

Still in the domain of doubt of fact, the glossator recognized the existence of instances wherein a rendered judgment nonetheless brought prejudice to someone. This situation, however, arose only when danger loomed for the soul. The glossa at this point referred to c. 3, X, *de sponsalibus*, IV, 1, where the classical doctrine of tutiorism was applied in all its rigidity to a question of marriage.

[8] De ecclesiarum consecrationibus quotiens dubitatur, ut nec certa scriptura, nec testes existunt, a quibus consecratio sciatur, absque ulla dubitatione scitote eas esse sacrandas; nec talis trepidatio facit iterationem, quoniam non monstratur esse iteratum quod nescitur factum.—C. 16, D. I, *de cons.*, VI Pars, § 1; JK, n. 878.

[9] Cf. Hinschius, *Decretales Pseudo-Isidorianae et Capitula Angilramni* (Leipzig: Tauchnitz, 1863), p. 687, where this letter is listed among the pseudo-Isidorian decretals.

[10] Parvulos, qui parentibus subtracti sunt, et an baptizati an non, ignoratur, ut hos baptizare debeas secundum Patrum traditiones, si non fuerit qui testificetur, ratio poscit.—C. 110, D. IV, *de cons.*; JK, n. 2174.

[11] "Nam in talibus certius est tenendum."—*Glossa* ad v. *ratio, loc. cit.*

Wherever the element of danger for the soul was encountered, the glossators and commentators continually adverted to this text as furnishing the fundamental principle for their position.[12] This text studied the case of a youth who had married a girl not yet seven years of age, and had possibly attempted to consummate the union. Subsequently, he married the girl's aunt, whereupon the doubt arose: was he really wed to the aunt or the niece. Pope Eugene III (1145-1153) decided that the man had to be separated from the aunt for two reasons: the good of the Church and the doubt that the first marriage might be valid. In his study of this topic, the glossator enunciated the main principle which prompted the pope's action: in questions of doubt, that which proved the more tenable was to be maintained.[13] Panormitanus (Nicolaus de Tudeschis, + 1453), in his commentary on this passage, clearly brought to light the necessity of standing for the more secure in doubtful matters when there threatened any danger for the soul.[14]

In the Decretals there are at least seven other instances in which the doctrine of tutiorism was upheld. These are cases concerned with moral problems, the validity of the sacraments, or the exercise of Orders. Pope Lucius III (1181-1185) held that, as long as the death of a spouse remained doubtful, it was unlawful to attempt to remarry.[15] Clement III (1187-1191) maintained the same position in stating that, even if husbands had been absent for many years, their wives could not remarry until certain news of the death of the husband had been received.[16]

12 "Quia igitur in his quae dubia sunt, quod certius existimamus, tenere debemus."

13 "Sic ergo patet quod in dubiis semper certius est tenedum."—*Glossa*, ad v. *dubia*, c. 3, X, *de sponsalibus et matrimoniis*, IV, 1.

14 "In concernentibus periculum animae debemus in dubiis semper tenere quod certius est et quod sine periculo animae explicari potest."—*Omnia quae extant Commentaria in Decretales* (Venetiis, 1588), Lib. IV, tit. I, c. 3.

15 "Sed in re dubia certius et modestius est huiusmodi nuptiis abstinere." —C. 2, X, *de secundis nuptiis*, IV, 21.

16 "Non possunt ad aliorum consortium canonice convolare . . . donec certum nuntium recipient de morte virorum."—C. 19, X, *de sponsalibus et matrimoniis*, IV, 1.

A priest had chastised a man; shortly thereafter the indivdual had died; a doubt then arose whether the death had followed from the wounds suffered at the hands of the priest. Clement ruled that the priest was not to engage in the ministry, since in questions of doubt the more secure line of action was to be followed.[17] Innocent III (1198-1216) judged that, if a priest was in doubt whether or not he was excommunicated, he should refrain from the administration of the sacraments, and this always for the same motive: the security of action.[18] The same pope commanded that a priest, when it was found that he was unbaptized, should be baptized and reordained, for such a matter could not be left to chance, and the surer course had to be pursued.[19] Innocent repeated the ideas of Clement III regarding an act in which a priest had been engaged and from which death had ensued. Doubt left it possible that the priest might have murdered the man, and because of this the priest had to desist from his sacerdotal functions. It was safer to abstain in this case, said the pontiff, because otherwise great harm might arise.[20] Honorius III (1216-1227) reiterated the same doctrine in the case of homicide, and for the same reasons.[21] Clement V (1305-1314), after a century which saw the flowering of the ecclesiastical sciences, nonetheless repeated the very principles his predecessors had advanced.[22]

[17] "Cum in dubiis semitam debeamus eligere tutiorem."—C. 12, X, *de homicidio*, V, 12. Vide etiam C. 39, D. L.

[18] "Quia in dubiis via est eligenda tutior."—C. 5, X, *de clerico excommunicato deposito, vel interdicto ministrante*, V, 27.

[19] "In hoc dubitabili casu, quod tutius est sequentes."—C. 3, *de presbytero non baptizato*, III, 43.

[20] "In hoc dubio tamquam homicida debet haberi secerdos . . . cum in hoc casu cessare sit tutius quam temere celebrare."—C. 18, X, *de homicidio*, V, 12.

[21] "Cum sit consultius in huiusmodi dubio abstinere quam temere celebrare."—C. 24, X, *de homicidio*, V, 12.

[22] "Nos itaque, qui in sinceris horum conscientiis delectamur, attendentes quod in his, quae animae salutem respiciunt, ad vitandos graves remorsus conscientiae pars securior est tenenda, dicimus . . . "—C. 1, *de verborum significatione*, V, 11, in Clem.

It is stranger yet to note that the glossator commented on each different text by direct reference to others of the same nature. For the observer there could but emerge the sensation of being hemmed in at all times in consequence of this continual return to the same areas wherein the subject was encountered. This, too, helps to create the strong impression that tutiorism alone held sway in the application of law. However, in a subsequent article, it will be shown that this did not apply to the strictly penal field.[23] Then, too, Bernard of Parma (+ 1266), the glossator, was a man of his time. The great theologians of the thirteenth century, Alexander of Hales, St. Albert the Great, St. Thomas Aquinas, always advanced the tutioristic solution when resolving problems of doubt of conscience in which there existed danger for the soul.[24] In other words, tutiorism prevailed, because no other doctrine had been evolved to solve the practical doubts that each day arose.

Article 2. Departures from Tutioristic Principles in the *Corpus Iuris Canonici*

Section I. Departures in Penal Matters

The area of penal matters offers an interesting sidelight to an altogether regular pattern as regards doubt of fact. In this re-

23 "Sic ergo patet, quod in dubiis semper certius est tenendum . . . et iam de homicidio, ad audientiam (i.e., c. 12, X, *de homicidio,* V, 12)."—*Glossa,* ad v. *dubia,* c. 3, X, *de sponsalibus et matrimoniis,* IV, 1.

"Et ita propter dubium praesumitur pro matrimonio, quod fieri debet, supra c. 3, X, *de sponsalibus et matrimoniis,* IV, 1."—*Glossa* ad v. *non deneget,* c. 2, X, *de secundis nuptiis,* IV, 21.

"Sic infra (c. 2, X, *de secundis nuptiis,* IV, 21) . . . "—*Glossa* ad v. *donec certium nuntium,* c. 19, X, *de sponsalibus et matrimoniis,* IV, 1.

"Sic supra (c. 3, X, *de sponsalibus et matrimoniis,* IV, 1), et infra (c. 16, X, *de homicidio,* V, 12 et c. 9, X, *de clerico excommunicato,* V, 27)."—*Glossa* ad v. *in dubiis,* c. 12, X, *de homicidio,* V, 12.

"Sic supra (c. 3, X, *de sponsalibus et matrimoniis,* IV, 1, et c. 16, X, *de homicidio,* V, 12, et c. 12, X, *de homicidio,* V, 12, et c. 24, X, *de homicidio,* V, 12), ubi de hoc."—*Glossa* ad v. *in dubiis,* c. 5, X, *de clerico excommunicato, V,* 27.

24 Lottin, *Psychologie et Morale au XIIe et XIIIe Siècles* (3 tomes in 4 vols., Louvain: Abbaye du Mont-César et Gembloux: J. Duculot, 1942-1949), II, 407-415.

spect, it must be noted that, at times, a double standard of evaluation was set up, permitting a practical mitigation of the tutioristic doctrine. A vivid instance of this twofold aspect was revealed by Clement III when he was called upon to determine whether or not a priest had incurred an irregularity. This priest had attempted to chastise some member of his family with a belt to which a knife was attached. In the course of the punishment, the knife slipped out of its shield and somewhat wounded the victim. The injured party recovered from the wound, but shortly thereafter, stricken with some infirmity, died. A doubt arose: did the victim die as a result of the wound? Clement III solved the problem by stating the fundamental tutioristic principle: the priest must refrain from the exercise of the ministry. However, the pope further enjoined that, once the proper penance was discharged minor orders might again be exercised.[25]

The glossator, in this connection, brought to the fore the classical texts of tutiorism; nonetheless, he added another cardinal principle of procedure: in a doubtful case it is impossible to mete out a definite sentence.[26] The decretalists engaged in a solid study of this text, and brought to light the underlying jurisprudence which helped to solve the problem. Ioannes Andreae (+ 1348), in connection with the interpretation of this irregularity, set forth a twofold rule. The first held that, if the facts were of a doubtful nature, neither a superior nor a judge could declare anyone irregular; the second declared that, in such cases, each and everyone should consider himself as laboring under an irregularity, or follow the dictates of his conscience.[27]

[25] C. 12, X, *de homicidio,* V, 12.

[26] "Et in re dubia certa non potest ferri sententia,"—c. 74, C. XI, q. 3, et dictum Gratiani ad c. 11, C. XXX, q. 5; "...Unde quandoque propter ambiguum duplicitatis imponitur poenitentia, supra c. 3, X, *de his qui filios occiderunt,* V, 10."—*Glossa* ad v. *in dubiis,* c. 12, X, *de homicidio,* V, 12.

[27] "In dubio, quae interpretatio facienda (est) de irregularitate. Nam circa hanc materiam duas regulas trado. Prima est quod in dubio nec magister nec iudex debet aliquem iudicare irregularem . . . Secunda est quod in dubio unusquisque debet se irregularem reputare . . . Ergo quamvis ipsum irregularem non iudicem de crimine; si tamen a me petat consilium, in dubio consulam quod se irregularem debeat reputare . . . vel ad minus

Panormitanus followed the same line of thought in his commentary on this passage. He clearly distinguished between the judicial field and that of the conscience, and, as a result, presented substantially the same solution as that advanced by Ioannes Andreae.[28]

In penal matters, more benign norms were applied; there was need of positive proof in order to condemn an accused person. It was basic that a judge could not sentence a man on dubious evidence.[29] Already the *Decree of Gratian* had announced the principle that it is grave and unseemly to pronounce a definite sentence in a doubtful matter.[30] Pope Gregory the Great (590-604) had occasion to put into use such jurisprudential tenets. He upbraided a bishop who quickly punished clerics without giving full ear to the charge. There was need for the bishop to search after the truth, and only then, if the matter warranted it, to resort to punishment.[31] In another situation, a bishop had lived rather loosely before his episcopal consecration. After the consecratory ceremony, rumors of concubinage reached Gregory's ear. The Pope, not duly informed about the facts of the case, did not condemn the man, but left it to his conscience to desist

ubi non est infamatus, est suae conscientia relinquendus."—*In Quinque Libros Decretalium Novella Commentaria* (Venetiis, 1581), Lib. V, tit. XII, c. 12.

28 "Unde sic distinguerem, quod in foro contentioso, ubi agitur de poena imponenda pro irregularitate contracta, non debet quis in dubio reputari irregularis: quia pure tunc agitur ad poenam . . . Aut agitur in foro poenitentiali ad imponendam poenitentiam, et in dubio debet potius reputari irregularis, quia in foro poenitentiae semper tutior pars est eligenda, licet videatur durior, quia in illa parte nullum subest periculum."—*Omia Quae Exstant Commentaria in Decretales*, Lib. V, tit. XII, c. 12.

29 "Quamvis vera sint quaedam, tamen iudici non sunt credenda, nisi certis indiciis demonstrentur."—C. 75, C. XI, q. 3.

30 "Grave satis est et indecens, ut in re dubia certa detur sententia."—C. 74, C. XI, q. 3.

31 "Si quid vero de quocumque clerico ad aures tuas pervenerit, quod te iuste possit offendere, facile non credas, nec ad vindictam te res accendat incognita; sed praesentibus ecclesiae tuae senioribus diligenter veritas est perscrutanda, et tunc, si qualitas rei poposcerit, canonica districtio culpam feriat delinquentis."—C. 23, D. LXXXVI.

from the ministry, if the rumors were founded, because of the peril to which his soul was exposed.[32]

Therefore, if anyone was in doubt whether he had incurred an irregularity or an excommunication, he was to consider himself irregular or excommunicated. The scene had shifted from the external forum to the sphere of the conscience. Nonetheless, the glossator maintained the presumption that a man was deserving and good until proved otherwise, even in the face of the previously enumerated principle. This brings to admirable light the distinction which obtained between the court and the conscience.[33]

Hostiensis (Henricus de Segusio, + 1271), in at least two different passages of his commentary, examined the problem. He insisted that in doubtful matters the more benign interpretation was imperative in judicial procedure, but this could not be brought to bear in the domain of the conscience, where security was of the very essence. A judge could not act as if he were certain, when in fact a doubt was present, and consequently could not proceed to the act of condemnation.[34] Hence, again, tutior-

[32] "Sed quia in rebus ambiguis absolutum non debet esse iudicium, hoc tuae conscientiae committendum eligimus. Qua de re, si in sacro ordine constitutus eius te recolis permixtione maculum, sacerdotii honore deposito ad ministrandum nullo modo praesumas accedere: sciturus in animae tuae periculo te ministrare, et Deo nostro te sine dubio reddere rationem, si huius sceleris conscius in eo quo ex ordine celans veritatem permanere volueris."—C. 7, D. XXXIII.

[33] "Nota quemlibet praesumi dignum, nisi probetur indignus, et de quolibet praesumendum est bonum, nisi probetur contrarium. Sed contra videtur: quia praesumitur non idoneus, nisi probetur idoneus, et in dubio praesumitur quis excommunicatus. Hoc generale est, ut ubi periculum animae vertitur, praesumatur in deteriorem partem . . . sed licet videatur deterior, tamen melior et tutior est . . . Alias circa iudicia potius praesumitur iustum, vel bonum, quam e converso."—*Glossa* ad v. *aestimare*, c. 1, X, *de scrutinio*, I, 12.

[34] "Haec autem benigna interpretatio in foro contentioso locum habet, nam in foro animae non est acceptandum id quod videtur homini benignius, sed quod animae securius est."—*In Decretalium Commentaria* (Venetiis, 1581), Lib. II, tit. XX, c. 16.

"Et est argumentum quod dubia in meliorem partem interpretari debemus . . . et quod promptiores debemus esse ad absolvendum quam ad

ism obtained in the field of one's eternal salvation, but was rejected in the case of procedure when only doubtful proof was adduced. This seems to bear out the conclusion that the strict domain of the conscience was the sole area wherein tutiorism held sway. In the field of procedure, when penalties had been imposed as a result of court action, much more than a doubt was postulated for the emergence of an obligation; evidence of a clear-cut and positive type was a prime requisite before a condemnation could be imposed. This is also clear from the fact that in Clement III's case, i.e., c 12, X, *de homicidio*, V, 12, the cleric was not even deposed.

SECTION II. TUTIORISM DOES NOT SOLVE ALL DOUBTS IN THE CORPUS IURIS CANONICI

While it has been shown that tutiorism proved to be a highly practical norm for solving doubts in many moral and juridical quarters, texts were also adduced which sought to demonstrate that in penal matters a certain mitigation of this rigidity found favor in the Decretals. However, the popes never felt exclusively committed to tutiorism as the sole key to the solution of doubt. On the contrary, instances are found which, of necessity, preclude the possibility of asserting that medieval law and ethics were bound by ironclad ties to this system of morality. Indeed, several passages from the Decretals resolve problems by employing principles which are at wide variance with tutiorism. These principles are not expressly stated, and, for that reason, it seems advisable to examine each case separately in order to determine, if possible, what grounds are common to all.

Before setting out to study the Decretals, one could with benefit consider a case of doubt as reflected in the *Decree of Gratian.* St. Augustine was called upon to determine the guilt of one who goes to war when the justice of such an undertaking is questionable. Even if war is waged for unjust reasons, he averred, the men may fight and obey orders; if there arise any doubt as to the propriety of these orders, the soldier is innocent, and the

---

condemnandum . . . quod verum est in iudicio contentioso . . . in quo non debet iudex aliquis se certum reddere, ubi certus non est, nec dubitare, ubi dubitandum non est . . . "—*Op. cit.*, Lib. V, tit. XIX, c. 19.

leader is the one really guilty of the offenses.[35] The solution, according to the glossa, was premised on the fact that, if a matter be of a dubious nature, one must always obey one's superior, who is the one answerable for his orders.[36]

While this pronouncement might conceivably smack of tutiorism in that it might seem safer to accept the judgment of one's superior, it did not necessarily follow that the superior, especially one who willingly engaged in unjust warfare, would take into consideration such items as the morality of his commands. Hence, to all intents and purposes, the tutioristic practice was conveniently laid to one side, while the guilt was heaped on the superior, because he was presumed to be the source of the evil.

Lucius III (+ 1185) was asked to appraise a marriage which had been contracted apart from the ascertainment if the spouse of one of the new partners was really deceased. The pope first established the general principle that such unions must not be permitted until certain proof be had of the death of the original partner. Nonetheless, if this had not been observed, and doubt remained concerning the death of the prior spouse, the partner was not to refuse his marital obligations, but had to refrain from requesting the reciprocal duty. However, if proof was brought forth that the first partner was still alive, the man had to return to her.[37] This practical arrangement was a far cry from the traditional doctrine.[38] It is true that Lucius III circumscribed the limits wherein such a solution might be arrived at, but this was definitely contrary to the established usage. While there was still a touch of tutiorism in the demand that the party of such a previous union could not, under any circumstance, ask for the marital act, it was nonetheless a departure from the ordinary doctrine in that it permitted him to honor the request of the new partner.

Celestine III (+ 1198) solves in a novel fashion the problem of impotence in marital relations. The couple were bidden to

[35] C. 4, C. XXII, q. 1.

[36] *Glossa,* ad v. *iniquitas,* c. 4, C. XXII, q. 1.

[37] C. 2, X, *de secundis nuptiis,* IV, 21.

[38] C. 19, X, *de sponsalibus et matrimoniis,* IV, 1.

cohabit for three years from the date of the marriage. If after that period no consummation was achieved, the wife could petition for a judgment which, when favorably rendered, allowed her to wed another.[39] Again a solution was offered that was fraught with danger. Even while the tutioristic principle of sustaining the validity of the marriage did underlie the pope's response, the peril of onanism or of collusion for the purpose of ending the union was very much present, and proved contrary to the norms of the safer course to be followed.

Innocent III (+ 1216), on several occasions, departed from the established rule of tutiorism in his responses concerning doubtful matters. A Carthusian had been ordained a subdeacon. Shortly thereafter he learned that the ordaining prelate had often committed the sin of simony. For this reason he feared to exercise his Order and refused to be promoted to higher Orders by the same bishop. At best, it was only doubtful that the bishop had been simoniacal in raising him to the subdiaconate. The pope answered that he could safely serve as a subdeacon, but that he was not to ascend to higher Orders against his conscience; however, if he rid himself of his scrupulosity, then the road to subsequent ordinations would be open to him.[40]

There is a very definitely tutioristic pattern in one portion of Innocent's answer: one must not act against one's conscience. Yet, there was a new outlook regarding the matter of exercising Orders which one might have simoniacally received. As a rule, an irregularity was attached to the recipient under such conditions, and the basic principle which then obtained was that one refrain from the exercise of the Orders received. Here the pope did not hesitate; doubt or no doubt, the Carthusian could safely act as a subdeacon. No legal principle was invoked in support of the contention. The Decretalists blissfully ignored the innovation, and extended themselves to show the need of correcting a doubtful or erroneous conscience.[41]

In another passage, Innocent III was confronted with a doubt concerning an impediment that was discovered only after a mar-

[39] C. 5, X, *de frigidis, de malificiatis, et impotentia caeundi,* IV, 15.

[40] C. 35, X, *de simonia,* V, 3.

[41] Hostiensis and Panormitanus, Lib. V, tit. III, c. 35.

riage had taken place. What was to be done? A distinction was in order, so answered the pope: either one or the other spouse certainly was aware of this, or, if not certain, nevertheless believed that the impediment possibly existed. In the first alternative, the knowing partner was subject to excommunication and had to cease all marital relations. In the other alternative, one had again to distinguish: either this knowledge was obtained from a weak and negligible source, or it came as a probable and discerning information. In the former instance, the acquired knowledge counted for nothing, and normal conjugal relations were to be resumed upon the bishop's advice. In the latter, since the matter was not clear and evident, the one who was aware that possibly an impediment existed could not request the marital act, although he could engage in it upon the request of his partner to do so.[42] Here again is found a new idea intermingled with a characteristically tutioristic answer. Indeed, it was accounted permissible to act in the face of probable and obscure knowledge. While it is true that this was a departure from the ordinary solution, the innovation does not strike one until one reads Panormitanus on this point. According to him, to know and to hold an opinion were two very distinct facets of the mind. Knowledge looked to certitude, but opinion could be lured by the uncertain and, at times, by fallacy.[43] The Pope, in this case, considered legitimate the cohabitation of this couple, whose marriage was perhaps vitiated with an impediment; yet, all the while Pope Innocent stressed the principles of tutiorism, which limited the exercise of the marital prerogatives on the side of the parties.

There had arisen a situation wherein a wife impugned the validity of her marriage by reason of consanguinity in the fourth degree, then a diriment impediment for which a dispensation could not be granted. Her husband sought to have her return to him. Confronted with the problem, Innocent III, in spite of the previous tutioristic responses given by his predecessors, and mindful of the moral perils involved, nonetheless ordered the

[42] C. 44, X, *de sententia excommunicationis*, V, 39.

[43] "Nota 1. ex textu quod aliud est scire, aliud est credere. Nam scientia habet se ad certum, et credulitas ad incertum et quandoque continet in se falsum."—Lib. V, tit. XXXIX, c. 44.

judge to have the woman sent back to her husband if her proofs were not manifestly evident. In other words, the judge was instructed to disregard the domain of the woman's conscience and the consideration of the tutioristic aspect. He had to render a decision for the external forum according to the procedural norms, even if this judgment conflicted with the woman's conscience, and the woman was to be compelled to accept the court's decision under pain of ecclesiastical censure.[44]

It is obviously clear that Innocent did not particularly wish to contain the problem within tutioristic lines: he preferably desired a solution consistent with the standards of procedure as practiced in the ecclesiastical courts, and he so instructed the judge. Better yet, he went so far as to oblige the woman to abide by the court's sentence, even if the latter clashed with her moral views.

A bishop had, without proper authorization, made a vow to visit the Holy Land. In so doing he had exposed himself to the danger of violating the law of residence. As a result it became doubtful that the vow was licit. However, in his solution of the difficulty, Innocent did not appeal to tutiorism as a practical rule; he argued that while the vow had to be fulfilled, the object of the vow was to be changed, so that when the new object of the vow was completely carried out, the obligation would cease entirely.[45] Tutiorism would have required of the bishop the pursuit of the safer course, that is, the complete fulfilment of his vow as originally taken. Nonetheless, Innocent safeguarded the vow by simply substituting a new object that supplanted the assumed obligation. Hence, without any appeal to tutiorism, the pope settled a vexing problem for the bishop.

What was the principle underlying these solutions? At first glance, it could appear that no principle whatever was involved. As a matter of fact, none was advanced in substantiation of the papal answers. However, it is eminently possible that the basis was simply the "principle of possession." This principle apparently applied to the cases wherein there was question of

[44] C. 13, X, *de restitutione spoliatorum,* II, 13.

[45] C. 7, X, *de voto et voti redemptione,* III, 34.

matrimony or of holy Orders.[46] Indeed, the popes rigidly supported the validity of the marriages and the orders therein discussed; they required, especially in matrimonial matters, a definite proof to the contrary before declaring such unions null and void.[47]

This principle of possession, then, seemed to plant the root out of which could spring a presumption sustaining the validity of the marriage or the Orders. The purpose of the presumption was the engendering of a practical certitude by which people could guide their everyday lives. It did not eliminate the speculative doubt that still lurked in their minds: they could still be affected with concern about the objective honesty of their actions. Nonetheless, in the face of this possibility, the Roman pontiffs endeavored through this method to preserve the existing order of society. Presumptions did not invariably spell out the last word in a legal difficulty; indeed, juridical evidence alone, if clear and cogent, sufficed to overcome the stringency of the presumption, and to open the road to a new legal determination of the case.

Presumptions were not constituted as direct norms of morality, such as the natural or ecclesiastical law could supply. Rather, they were of service through their indirect approach to moral and legal problems. They entered into play when an individual was confronted with a doubt as to the propriety of an action which he felt it his duty to perform here and now, or when society was called upon to resolve a doubt which might wreak havoc with its structure. The indirect approach, or the reflex principle as it came to be known to later theologians, was not commonly employed at the time of the Decretals. It was the

[46] C. 2, X, *de secundis nuptiis*, IV, 21; c. 44, X, *de sententia excommunicationis*, V, 39; c. 5, X, *de frigidis*, IV, 15; c. 13, X, *de restitutione spoliatorum*, II, 13; c. 35, X, *de simonia*, V, 3.

[47] ". Quodsi post hoc de prioris coniugis vita constiterit, relictis adulterinis complexibus ad priorem coniugem revertatur."—C. 2, X, *de secundis nuptiis*, IV, 21.

" Quodsi non habeat probationes in continenti paratas, sed dilationes expectat longiores . . . ad restitutionem plenariam ecclesiastica debt censura compelli."—C. 13, X, *de restitutione spoliatorum*, II, 13.

C. 5, X, *de frigidis*, IV, 15, required a three-year trial period in order to safeguard the marriage when a doubt regarding impotence had arisen.

theologians and canonists who developed the concept, and the use of it became prevalent shortly thereafter.

Article 3. The *Corpus Iuris Canonici* Paves the Way for the Principle: *lex dubia non obligat*

Jurisprudence, as encountered in the Decretals, did not contain any provision similar to that offered by the Code of Canon Law. "*Lex dubia non obligat*", as a principle governing legislation encompassed by the *Corpus Iuris Canonici,* was unthinkable for the medieval mind. The preceding articles reveal the close scrutiny with which doubtful facts and laws were examined for the purpose of making them conform to existing legal patterns. In the domain of the conscience, tutiorism held sway as a rule. Because of the odious character of penal and procedural matters, facts of a dubious nature were irrelevant for the establishing of guilt before the courts and for the punishing of the accused. There now remains the task of considering the situation which obtained when the law itself was doubtful in some way.

Gratian conceived the idea of a systematic concordance to effectuate harmony in legislation. Surely the discordance which prevailed in ecclesiastical law must have definitely been a source of constant annoyance, and the legislation which had accumulated through the centuries must have offered a rich lode of doubtful laws. However, Gratian could never hope to succeed completely in his endeavor because of the high esteem in which the authorities were held. It was even thought in the twelfth century that the Fathers of the Church had received special inspiration from the Holy Ghost.[48] A similar opinion was recognized concerning the authority of the Councils. This led to vigorous efforts to produce a harmonization of incongruous materials which defied such treatment. As a practical consequence, the question of the *dubium iuris* never entered into consideration, because it was essential that disparate laws be organized in a harmonious body.

[48] De Ghellinck, *Le Mouvement Theologique au XIIe siecle* (2. ed., Bruges: Editions "de Tempel"; Bruxelles: L'Edition Universelle; Paris: Desclée-De Brouwer, 1948), pp. 474-480.

Furthermore, the description of law, as put forth by St. Isidore (560-636) and as then understood, ruled out all doubts of law even as a possibility. Indeed, the Spanish prelate had unequivocally stated that law must be clear.[49] However, it may prove helpful to recall the explanations which were offered in this connection. The problem was never envisaged from the angle that a law may or may not be clear: clarity was always a requisite of law. The issue at stake centered on whether clarity was a necessary property of law or whether it was a condition of law. If clarity was a necessary property of law, it necessarily flowed from the essence of law. As a result, in the absence of such a constituent factor, doubtful legislation could not possibly exist as a binding force, and would therefore be inane. If, on the other hand, clarity was simply a condition of law, not requisite for the validity of its inner structure, but very helpful in achieving the perfection of law, then the presence or the absence of clarity would in no way disrupt the substance of a law, and its obligatory force would be maintained.

St. Thomas Aquinas (1225-1274) consecrated an article of his *Summa Thelogiae* to the study of the conditions for a true law. His approach to the problem was metaphysical in character. All means, he stated, must of necessity be proportionate to the end. Human law, being a means, must therefore be proportionate to its end. Now, the purpose of human law is the utility of mankind; hence human law must needs be in proportion with the utility of mankind. But, among other properties, only a clear law is proportionate to the utility of men. This clarity is called for because of the great harm which might be engendered by the law itself, and since law is enacted with a view of assuring the welfare of all, everything must be done to render ineffectual the possibility of harm which might conceivably arise out of dubious legislation.[50]

[49] "Erit autem lex honesta, iusta, possibilis, secundum naturam, secundum patriae consuetudinem, loco temporique conveniens, necessaria, utilis, manifesta quoque, ne aliquid per obscuritatem inconveniens (Roman Correctors: in captionem) contineat, nullo privato commodo sed pro communi civium utilitate conscripta."—C. 2, D. IV.

[50] Ia IIae, q. 95, a. 3.

The mind of St. Thomas was definite: law must be clear. But, nowhere in his treatise of law did he state that clarity is a necessary property of law, nor did he aver that it is required for the perfection of law. One or the other position can be derived from his treatment. Had he pursued this path, he might have discovered the principle, *"lex dubia non obligat."* However, St. Thomas was a man of his time, and the juridical doctrine which then prevailed in respect of the *dubium iuris* called for recourse to the legislator for an explanation *" nè res pereat."*

The Decretals reveal an analogous passage which maintains that pontifical legislation must contain nothing obscure or ambiguous.[51] The *glossa,* in this respect, remarked that a law must contain no obscurity, lest it lead into a snare. Indeed, its function is to prevent such an eventuality.[52] This also necessarily bears out the need of clarity in legislation. Panormitanus, in his commentary of the same passage, maintained the urgency of clarity for fear that, if law be difficult to grasp, one might fall prey to some danger. However, he likened a law if it was very doubtful to a practical case of ignorance, and summarily declared that in such occurrences one was excused by reason of ignorance of law.[53] Whether or not one agrees with the jurisprudence of Panormitanus is immaterial; he did hold the necessity of clarity in legislation.

51 " Quoniam constitutio Apostolicae sedis omnes adstringit, et nihil debet obscurum vel ambiguum continere . . . "—C. 13, X, *de constitutionibus,* I, 2.

52 " Lex enim sive constitutio debet esse honesta et iusta, et nullam obscuritatem continere debet: et talis ut traditur c. 2, D. IV, ne per obscuram constitutionem in laqueum incidamus. Nemini, nota, debemus laqueum iniicere . . . nec debet nos inducere per legem obscuram vel dubiam ad id a quo nos cohibere debet . . . et qui me defendere debet, non debet me impugnare."—*Glossa,* ad v. *ambiguum,* c. 13, X, *de constitutionibus,* I, 2.

53 " Nota 2 quod constitutio debet esse clara quoad litteram et quoad mentem . . . Ratio colligitur ex textu ne ex difficultate intellectus legis quis incidat in promptum periculum. Unum tamen scias quod ubi lex est multum dubia, excusatur quis a iuris ignorantia."—*Omnia Quae Extant Commentaria in Decretales,* Lib. I, tit. II, cap. 13.

Pope John XXII (1316-1334) expressed analogous ideas in his Bull *Quoniam nulla* (October 25, 1317). This document, which served as a foreword to the Clementine Constitutions, brought to light the pontiff's views on the necessity but also the difficulty of legislating clearly. He blamed the complexity of human nature for the failure of law to foresee completely the cases wherein existing legislation would be unable to alleviate the situation and, as a result, be revoked in doubt. Hence there was need for authority to dispel obscurity and ambiguity in law, to solve difficulties stemming from law, and to enact provisions for the handling of these affairs. This Pope Clement V (1305-1314) endeavored to do in his Constitutions.[54]

It seems that John XXII entertained the opinion that a compliance with law could not always be urged when, because of circumstances, a doubt arose which rendered difficult the application of law. Then, too, he held it as a need for new legislation to clarify the old and to deal with new problems. His stand was definitely a confirmation of the opinion that law must be clear. While it is true that he gave assent to a view which calls for new laws to dispel obscurity and doubt, he nonetheless implicitly paved the way for the reflex principle: *lex dubia non obligat.*

The conclusion to be derived from this short conspectus definitely bears out the necessity of clarity in law. While it is not evident that the doctrine of doubt of law directly stems from these considerations, they nonetheless served as a premise from which future writers would derive the basic ideas which have obtained full approval today.

Another area which had a wide influence in shaping the development of the point at issue was the one concerned with the relations of law and liberty. In the *Corpus Iuris Canonici,* the position which liberty enjoys with regard to the law is always predicated on the clear distinction which obtains between the sphere of the conscience and the juridical domain. It has been shown that, whenever there arose a doubt that might expose one to the danger of sin, the safer course had to be followed. However, if this peril was averted, how did liberty fare in the face of the doubtful law?

[54] *Prooemium Clementinarum a Ioanne XXII confectum.*

In penal matters, jurisprudence, as found throughout the history of the Church and properly embodied in the ecclesiastical laws, has always held that liberty must prevail unless accusations can be proved both in law and in fact. This principle is borne out by pontifical letters written for the purpose of curbing undue rashness in the infliction of punishment. Gregory the Great (590-604) urged utmost prudence before bishops could proceed to punish clerics, and indicated the broad lines of procedure to be followed in this connection.[55] Pope Adrian I (772-795) decreed that excommunication should be inflicted on those who falsely charged bishops, priests and deacons with some crime and could not bring proof to substantiate the accusation.[56] There was also the case of a murder which had been committed by one of three clerics. A serious doubt had arisen regarding the identity of the culprit. In spite of the doubt, all were to be promoted to superior Orders. The glossator in commenting on this solution explained that, because of the doubt, viciousness is tolerated which otherwise would not be allowed.[57]

Similarly did Innocent III view the problem when he was called upon to prescribe a guide to determine the worthiness or unworthiness of a cleric called to major Orders. When one did not know that a cleric was unworthy, he answered, then such a

[55] "Si quid vero de quocumque clerico ad aures tuae pervenerit, quod te iuste possit offendere, facile non credas, nec ad vindictam te res accendat incognita; sed praesentibus ecclesiae tuae senioribus diligenter veritas est perscrutanda, et tunc, si qualitas rei poposcerit, canonica districtio culpam feriat delinquentis."—C. 23, D. LXXXVI; JK, n. 1529. This text is also found in c. 2, C. XV, q. 7; JK, n. 1191, but addressed to John, Bishop of Parma.

[56] "Si quis episcopum, aut presbyterum, aut diaconum falsis criminibus appetierit, et probare non potuerit, nec in fine dandam ei communionem censemus."—C. 4, C. II, q. 3.

[57] "Arguitur ad quaestionem ubi unus interfectus est ab uno de tribus, si dubitatur a quo, quod ratione dubitationis omnes debent promoveri, quia ratione dubitationis vitiosa et superflua tolerantur . . . Item est hic argumentum quod ratione connexionis permittitur quod alias non licet."—*Glossa* ad v. *triticum*, c. 22, C. XI, q. 3.

cleric was to be considered as worthy.[58] The gloss proved enlightening on this point, stating as it did that any one had to be presumed worthy, unless proof was adduced of his unworthiness, and in judicial matters also one was presumed just and good. However, in the domain of the conscience, the presumption stood rather for the worse in the sense that, in the event of doubtful excommunication, one was to consider oneself excommunicated.[59]

Outside penal matters, especially in the realm of procedure, liberty obtained against the law when the charge brought against the defendant was not proved. The text which best summarizes the juridical principle underlying this doctrine reads as follows: it is quite serious and unseemly that in a dubious matter a definite sentence be imposed.[60] This, however, was valid only for the external forum, so that the accused had yet to face the judgment of his conscience and to carry out its dictates regarding the safer course to follow.

It would be too broad an assumption to believe that the jurisprudence as engaged and employed in court activity was always clear-cut and definite. A long development led to a definitive procedure. This is perhaps best exemplified by the *glossa* attached to c. 7, D. XXXIII, where an attempt was made to solve the problem of doubt. In order properly to illustrate the commentary, it may prove helpful first to summarize the case. A priest had a concubine prior to his elevation to the episcopate.

58 "Unde in tali responsione aliquem peccare non credimus, dummodo contra conscientiam non loquatur, quia non simpliciter illum asserit esse dignum, sed in quantum humana fragilitas nosse sinit, quum illum, quem indignum esse non novit, dignum debeat aestimare . . . "—C. 1, X, *de scrutinio in ordine faciendo*, I, 12.

59 "Nota quemlibet praesumi dignum, nisi probetur indignus, et de quolibet praesumendum est bonum nisi probetur contrarium. Sed contra videtur: quia praesumitur non idoneus, nisi probetur idoneus, et in dubio praesumitur quis excommunicatus. Hoc generale est, ut ubi periculum animae vertitur, praesumitur in deteriorem partem . . . Alias circa iudicia potius praesumitur iustum vel bonum, quam e converso."—*Glossa* ad v. *aestimare*, c. 1, X, *de scrutinio in ordine faciendo*, I, 12.

60 "Grave satis est et indecens, ut in re dubia certa detur sententia."—C. 74, C. XI, q. 3, JK, n. 1779.

It was brought to the attention of Gregory the Great that this bishop had approached her since his consecration. Inasmuch as he had no certain knowledge of the matter, the pope did not excommunicate him, basing his stand on the principle: "*in rebus dubiis absolutum non debet esse iudicium*".[61]

In his commentary, the glossator began his treatment of ambiguity by distinguishing its various types: ambiguity of law, of fact, and of person. Thereafter he proceeded to show how each category was handled in procedure. When there arose a problem of ambiguity of law, one had to proceed by analogy to similar matters, and of such ambiguity was there question in c. 2, D. XIV. Yet, the *glossa* stated that a contrary view was put forth in that same passage. Doubt of fact was presented as the only ambiguity wherein a judicial sentence needed never to be handed down to the prejudice of anyone. There obtained always the endeavor, of course, to eliminate all danger for the soul.[62]

At first glance, it could appear that only ambiguity of fact could possibly benefit from the liberality of the court in the external forum, and that the principle "*in re dubia certa non datur sententia*" could apply only to doubt of fact. Nonetheless, the case for the *dubium iuris* was not lost. The text brought forward as opposed to the view of Pope Gregory, and given as an example in c. 2, D. XIV, was not precisely concerned with matters dubious, but with the relaxation of the law in certain instances. Therein Pope Leo I stated that whereas some laws may never be destroyed, there exist many others which can be

61 "Habuisse te concubinam manifesta veritate comperimus, et te illius criminis participationem habere de qua etiam contraria est quibusdam nata suspicio. Sed quia in rebus ambiguis absolutum non debet esse iudicium, hoc tuae conscientiae committendum eligimus . . . "—C. 7, D. XXXIII, JK, n. 1249.

62 "Sed D. XIV, "sicut" [c. 2] contra. Sed dicitur quod triplex est ambiguitas: ambiguitas iuris, ambiguitas facti, ambiguitas personae. Ubi ambiguitas iuris est, ibi de similibus ad similia proceditur, ut D. XX, "de libellis" [c. 1], et de tali ambiguitate loquitur illud c. [2], D. XIV, "sicut" . . . Sed ubi factum ambiguum est, tunc nunquam ferenda est sententia in alicuius praeiudicium . . . Tamen quandoque dubitatur de facto et fertur sententia in praeiudicium alterius . . . sed illud est propter periculum animae."—*Glossa* ad v. *ambiguis*, c. 7, D. XXXIII.

tempered, provided that they not contravene the Gospel and the decrees of the Fathers.[63] However, there are two instances in the Decretals dealing with petitory-possessory cases which clearly bear out that when the rights of the parties were obscure, it was customary to adjudge the issue favorably for the defendant.[64] This readiness to absolve, stated the glossator, obtained only in doubtful and obscure cases.[65]

Hostiensis, in his study of the rules of law, maintained that the more benign interpretation was to be followed, and that in doubtful matters the accused was to be acquitted, because this represented the milder form. He then proceeded to use the two preceding passages as the basis for his stand.[66] Panormitanus

[63] "Sicut quaedam sunt, quae nulla ratione convelli possunt, ita multa sunt, quae aut pro necessitate temporum aut pro consideratione aetatum oporteat temperari; illa semper conditione servata, ut in his, quae vel dubia fuerint aut obscura, id noverimus sequendum, quod nec praeceptis evangelicis contrarium, nec decretis sanctorum Patrum inveniatur adversum."—C. 2, D. XIV; JK, n. 544.

[64] "Quum autem super his fuisset diutius litigatum, quia legitime probata non fuerant quae petebantur ad monasterium pertinere, ab impetitione ipsius procuratorem tuum nomine tuo et Mediolanensis ecclesiae sententialiter duximus absolvendum, quoniam, quum obscura sunt iura partium, consuevit contra eum, qui petitor est, iudicari."—C. 6, X, *de fine instrumentorum*, II, 22, *in fine*.

"Quod si ambarum partium testes sint aeque idonei, possessoris testes praeferuntur, quum promptiora sint iura ad absolvendum quam ad condemnandum, praeterquam in liberali causa, in qua si utriusque partis testes aequales fuerint, pro libertate sententia proferetur."—C. 3, X, *de probationibus*, II, 19.

Also: "Item est hic argumentum quod dubia probatio non prodest ei qui eam inducit, sic supra [c. 8, X, *de probationibus*, II, 19]. Item argumentum quod in dubiis pro reo iudicari consuevit, supra [c. 6, X, *de fide instrumentorum*, II, 22, in fine] et supra [c. 3, X, *de probationibus*, II, 19], ff. *de regulis iuris, semper in dubiis*."—*Glossa* ad v. *benigne*, c. 16, X, *de testibus et attestationibus*, II, 20.

[65] "Quod hic dicitur et in similibus, locum habet in dubiis et obscuris."—*Glossa* ad v. *promptiora, in fine*, c. 3, X, *de probationibus*, II, 19.

[66] "Et benigniorem interpretationem sequi debemus in re dubia . . . Sic nota in dubiis absolvitur reus: quia illud est benignius, secundum "de fide instrumentorum, inter dilectos" [i.e., c. 6, X, *de fine instrumentorum*, II, 22], et secundum "de probationibus, ex litteris" [i.e., c. 3, X, *de proba-*

held a similar opinion when he reviewed the position which a judge had to assume when doubt arose. He examined every possible case of doubt and furnished a solution. He did, moreover, settle the difficulty which surged from the two points of view therein stated. If the law could be understood in many ways, or was uncertain, and a milder course remained available, that course was to be followed; if there was no milder course at hand, but similar legislation existed, then one was to proceed by analogy.[67]

As a result of these considerations, it can be concluded that the juridical positions of law and liberty, when confronted with a problem of doubt, would find liberty enjoying the favor of the legislator and of jurisprudence when the matter under examination did not offer any peril for the soul.

The Decretals provide a highly interesting statement as made by Gregory IX (1227-1241). In it this pope faced the problem of doubt in relation to usury. Three possibilities were envisaged, and solutions proper to each were offered. In the first instance, one was definitely looked upon as a usurer, if one accepted a fee for money lent. The second proposition dealt with one who gave money, in order that at a later date a quantity of grain, wine or oil would be delivered to him. This merchandise may then have a higher value, but at the time of the transaction there was a probable doubt that this might not necessarily be the case. The pontiff declared that, in the alleged circumstances, this act was not usury. One was also excused by reason of such doubt, if foodstuffs were sold under such conditions that one might receive at a definite time limit more for them than they were originally worth, provided, however, that at the time of the contract one had not formed an intention of selling.[68]

---

tionibus, II, 19]."—*In Decretalium Commentaria,* Lib. V, tit. XLI, c. 2. Cf. also Lib. II, tit. XIX, c. 3; Lib. II, tit. XX, c. 16; Lib. I, tit. VI, c. 16, where the same ideas were expressed.

67 "Aut est intellectus multiplex, vel incertus, et si appareat de benigniori via, illa est sequenda . . . Si non sit via benignior, tunc si est dare simile in aliis legibus, procedendum est de similibus ad similia . . ."—*Omnia Quae Extant Commentaria in Decretales,* Lib. I, tit. II, c. 1.

68 "Naviganti vel eunti ad nundinas certam mutuans pecuniae quantitatem, pro eo, quod suscipit in se periculum, recepturus aliquid ultra

This is a rare treatment of the question of doubt. Indeed, Gregory IX really furnished a rule of conduct to be followed when a doubt arose in cases of usury. He, undoubtedly the first, clearly and unequivocally proclaimed that a probable doubt excused from the sin of usury. The glossator, both in his study of the substance of the text and in his commentary on its important phrases, extended himself to show the jurisprudence underlying the pope's solutions. Doubt, he said, needed to be interpreted in the more favorable way; doubt excused from usury. But then, he interjected a note of caution: not every type of doubt would bring this about; only a probable doubt would do so.[69]

The *glossa* was quite extensive in its study of probable doubt. It examined all the possibilities wherein a businessman might find himself. If he was certain that the merchandise would have a lower price than the money received, he was definitely a usurer; if he was uncertain, he was excused, because both the buyer and the seller equally bore the convenience and the inconvenience arising out of the delay. It was here that the glossator injected the juridical principle that doubts had to be interpreted in the more favorable light, because one must be more readily disposed to absolve than to condemn. However, an objection was lodged against this stand, based on the premise that in such a doubt one should abstain from this sort of contract because of the danger involved for the soul. As a matter of fact, some could feign to doubt, and yet not doubt at all. Notwithstanding the strength of this objection for the medieval mind,

---

sortem, usurarius est censendus. Ille quoque, qui dat decem solidos, ut alio tempore totidem sibi grani, vini vel olei mensurae reddantur, quae licet tunc plus valeant, utrum plus vel minus solutionis tempore fuerint valiturae, verisimiliter dubitatur, non debet ex hoc usurarius reputari. Ratione huius dubii etiam excusatur, qui pannos, granum, vinum, oleum vel alias merces vendit, ut amplius, quam tunc valeant, in certo termino recipiat pro eisdem; si tamen ea tempore contractus non fuerat venditurus."—C. 19, X, *de usuris*, V, 19.

69 "Item dubia in meliorem partem sunt interpretanda. Item ratione dubii excusatur quis ab usura. Item non quodcumque dubium excusat ab usura, sed quando probabiliter dubitari potest."—*Casus glossae*, c. 19, X, *de usuris*, V, 19.

the glossator held that the matter should be left to one's conscience. Then, too, at times permission was granted for the doing of something in consequence of the doubt, which would otherwise have been refused, and in view also of the prudent doubt attending the case, one was excused from the law.[70]

The element of surprise in this gloss is the treatment accorded to the internal forum. Here no longer the hackneyed phrase of tutiorism was repeated: *pars tutior est sequenda,* but a definite development was reflected in the legal and moral solution of doubtful matters: *relinquendi sunt in talibus conscientiae suae.* The clear-cut exposition of discipline which was given by the pontiff was not solely a response to a difficulty. It tended to substantiate the idea that the *Corpus Iuris Canonici* contained, as in a seed, the legislation which came to fruition in the Code of Canon Law.

70 "Ergo si certum esset, quod tempore solutionis plus valerent, usurarius est censendus . . . Et ita propter dubium excusatur: quia tam emptor quam venditor aequaliter commodum et incommodum ex dilatione expectat . . . Item argumentum est hic quod dubia in meliorem partem interpretari debent . . . quia promptiores debemus esse ad absolvendum quam ad condemnandum . . . Sed contra quod potius in tali dubio abstinendum esset a talibus contractibus propter periculum. Qandoque nota aliqui fingunt se dubitare, ubi dubitatio non est, tamen relinquendi sunt in talibus conscientiae suae. Item argumentum quod ratione dubii aliquid permittitur, quod alias non licet . . . et ratione huius dubii excusatur . . ."—*Glossa* ad v. *verisimiliter dubitatur,* c. 19, X, *de usuris,* V, 19. Cf. also Hostiensis, Lib. V, tit. XIX, c. 19.

CHAPTER III

THE DOCTRINE OF DOUBT ACCORDING TO SUAREZ

FRANCIS SUAREZ (1548-1617) is the first great protagonist of probabilism. While it is true that Bartholomew de Medina (1527-1580) offered the first systematic exposition of the matter, it remained for the Spanish Jesuit to exhaust the principles of his predecessor and to bring them to their logical and ultimate conclusions. Where Medina was content to limit himself to the field of the conscience alone, Suarez struck out further; he considered doubt and opinion under the light of juridical and moral principles. The primary area of his works wherein the subject is studied are the *De Legibus* and the *De Bonitate et Malitia Actuum Humanorum*. However, it must be noted that the question of doubt in Canon Law is nowhere formally explored. The entire problem is viewed from the angle of positive human law, of which Canon Law is definitely a part. Doubt, as such, is not the object of definite and formal consideration in the *De Legibus;* it receives cursory mention in connection with principles of law which it might affect. As a result, the moral doctrine, as found in the *De Bonitate et Malitia Actuum Humanorum,* will offer Suarez's best treatment of doubt.

In a first article, doubt of law will be studied, and subsequently, doubt of fact.

ARTICLE 1. THE OBLIGATION OF A DOUBTFUL LAW

Suarez undertook his study with very general considerations relative to the nature of doubt. Doubt consisted in some perplexity of the mind and in the voluntary suspension of judgment. This suspension of judgment was further qualified. Indeed, a mere suspension of judgment did not suffice to induce doubt, for in that event one could possibly withhold assent from the most evident truths. This suspension of judgment had to result from the failure of the will, for the lack of a sufficient motive, to determine the intellect to adhere to one proposition. Consequently, doubt implied not only the absence of an act, but also the realization of the insufficiency of a motive for giving assent. This insufficiency could arise inasmuch as there did not exist any point of contact between two propositions, or inasmuch as the reasons were so equally probable that the intellect rightly withheld its assent and thus remained in doubt. It is the latter doubt which is the object of Suarez' treatment.[1]

A probable opinion, on the other hand, differed from a doubt in that it included a distinct assent to a proposition, with some fear regarding the other. An opinion was deemed probable also when it was founded on some reliable authority, or when it was not inconsistent with either the accepted tenets of the Church or the common doctrine of the doctors.[2]

Before setting out to discuss the effect of juridical doubt on the obligation of law, Suarez envisaged two important moral principles as delimiting the scope of the doubt of law. The first was concerned with practical doubt. Practical doubt could not ordinarily suffice to induce a morally honest action. Indeed, it was the accepted doctrine that such a doubt normally excluded the practical certitude that were essential for ethical conduct. Hence, when in practical doubt, one was always bound to forego the action in question because of the danger of sinning. The axiom, *in dubiis tutior pars est sequenda,* applied as a rule in the face of practical doubt. Yet, Suarez stated that in certain circumstancs it could become allowable for one to allay this doubt through the use of extrinsic principles or by way of appeal to some authority; it then became permissible to act.[3] The second principle dealt with speculative doubt. If one was in doubt regarding the knowledge of some speculative principle or of some matter from which the morality of an act seemed to depend, but nevertheless had a practical certitude of its honesty, this sufficed for ethical behaviour, so long as the honesty stood recognized as truly certain and as deriving from sure principles.[4]

[1] *De Bonitate et Malitia Actuum Humanorum,* Disp. XII, sect. V, n. 1. This work will hereafter be cited as *De Bon. et Mal. Act. Hum.*

[2] *De Bon. et Mal. Act. Hum.,* Disp. XII, sect. VI, n. 1.

[3] *De Bon. et Mal. Act. Hum.,* Disp. XII, sect. V, n. 2.

[4] *De Bon. et Mal. Act. Hum.,* Disp. XII, sect. V, n. 4.

The point at issue was this: how could one, in spite of this extrinsic doubt, arrive at the necessary practical certitude? Indeed there were principles: *tutior pars est sequenda; melior est conditio possidentis.* Both, however, offered grave disadvantages. To oblige men always to pursue the safer course would be unduly severe; and constantly to accede to a man's liberty would not always be safe. Hence there was the need for rendering a doubt involuntary and invincible through the use of due diligence in the effort to dispel it.[5] This task one could accomplish by adhering to the following rule: one could, upon a complete appraisal of the demands inherent in the nature of the matter, adopt whatever decision offered the least inconvenience. In order to demonstrate the application of this rule, Suarez developed his distinction between doubt of law and doubt of fact.[6]

It seems necessary at this juncture to indicate that, though Suarez examined the rôle of doubt of law in a purely moral treatise, he had recourse to juridical principles in the task of upholding his teaching. This does not mean that ethical truths were left unconsidered by Suarez, for that was truly and simply unthinkable in his case. Nonetheless, his philosophy of law, as embodied in the *De Legibus,* is a consideration to which he constantly adverted, as will be seen.

Doubt of law could relate to the existence, the obligation, the sense and the extent of a law. The doctrine of Suarez, in this connection, can be adequately stated in two general propositions. The first examines the existence and obligation of a law. When there is doubt relative to the existence and obligation of a law, the law does not bind. This is established in a twofold manner: from the very study of law itself, and from the position of the subject in regard to a doubtful law.

The investigation of law in its intimate nature reveals that a law does not bind, unless it be adequately promulgated and disclosed to men.[7] Indeed, if a law is to be perfectly constituted, it

[5] *De Bon. et Mal. Act. Hum.,* Disp. XII, sect. V, n. 5.

[6] *De Bon. et Mal. Act. Hum.,* Disp. XII, sect. V, n. 6.

[7] *Opera Omnia* (26 vols., Parisiis: Vives, 1856-1866), V & VI (*Tractatus de Legibus et Legislatore Deo,* 1856), Lib. I, cap. XI, nn. 3 & 6. This

must evince an effectively obligatory character. This cannot obtain until the law is promulgated. Hence, until it is promulgated a law is not perfectly constituted and accordingly is not a true law at all. The major premise is clear, for law sets up a compulsory standard of activity. The minor premise stems from the fact that law is a measure drawn up for the whole community; it must needs be proposed in such a way as to affect the entire community: and that is promulgation.[8] Furthermore, inasmuch as the obligation that attaches to a law reflects a burden if not also an anoyance, it cannot be urged unless it is known with certainty.[9]

Envisaged from the point of view of the subject, a doubt of law cannot create an obligation. The principle *in dubiis melior est conditio possidentis* obtains, and man retains his liberty.[10] It would, moreover, be an intolerable burden for man if before taking action he had to examine all the opinions pro and con. As a matter of fact, such a requirement to obtain complete knowledge for each human act would exceed the normal scope of the human mind.[11]

The second general consideration studies the sense and extent of a law. When it is clear that a law exists, but there arises some positive doubt regarding its signification or extent, the ordinary norm states that the law does not bind.[12]

It is certain, in view of the principles derived from the *De Legibus*, that the rules of interpretation should find application

---

work will hereafter be cited as *De Legibus*. Cf. also *De Bon. et Mal. Act. Hum.*, Disp. XII, sect. V, n. 7; *ibid.*, sect. VI, n. 7.

8 *De Legibus*, Lib. I, cap. XI, n. 3.

9 *De Bon. et Mal. Act. Hum.*, Disp. XII, sect. VI, n. 8.

10 *De Bon. et Mal. Act. Hum.*, Disp. XII, sect. V, n. 7.

11 *De Bon. et Mal. Act. Hum.*, Disp. XII, sect. VI, n. 8.

12 *De Bon. et Mal. Act. Hum.*, Disp. XII, sect. V, n. 7. In Disp. XII, sect. VI, n. 8, Suarez did not in any way distinguish between probable opinion as relating to the existence or as relative to the sense of a law. He merely referred to the lack of a proper promulgation and the intolerable burden imposed upon men. In Disp. XII, sect. V, n. 7, he stated that the same must be said in this case as in the case of the doubtful existence of a law, and indeed for the same reason.

when there is positive doubt concerning the sense of a law. The mind of the legislator must be sought, and law is presumed to be a valid norm from the very notion that an interpretation is being sought.[13] However, after a due examination of the antecedents, the subject matter, the purpose and the circumstances wherein the contemplated legislation came into being, if a clear signification is unobtainable, then there is no law. Indeed, the so-called law would not be indicative of the mind of the legislator, which is an essential item for a truly binding law.[14] Yet, Suarez remarked that recourse was to be interposed with the superior if that could easily be done, in order that he might dispel the doubt.[15] This statement did not militate against the validity of his original principle; it simply indicated the respect in which law must be held and the efforts that are required for the maintenance of the law whenever and wherever such efforts prove feasible.

The conclusion to be derived from this brief investigation is that Suarez furnished the first logical and articulate treatment with reference to the doubt of law. His position, in this respect, became the one that was later to be adopted in the Code of Canon Law.

Article 2. Law and Doubt of Fact

Doubt or probability of fact, according to Suarez, related to things or objects in contradistinction to doubt or probability of law which related to and affected the law itself. These objects he considered according to their nature or condition.[16] Whenever the question of doubt of fact arises, Suarez was no longer a probabilist. The principle, *lex dubia non obligat,* was not invoked for application. Indeed, there obtained generally that other principle from which a practically certain conscience was to be gained: *in dubiis tutior pars est sequenda.*

[13] *De Legibus,* Lib. VI, cap. I, n. 17.

[14] *De Legibus,* Lib. VI, cap. I, n. 11.

[15] *De Bon. et Mal. Act. Hum.,* Disp. XII, sect. V, n. 7.

[16] *De Bon. et Mal. Act. Hum.,* Disp. XII, sect. V, n. 6; sect. VI, n. 8.

The basic argument utilized in support of this contention may be thus summarized: the danger which is feared in the face of a doubtful fact is not affected in any way by one's opinion of it. In truth, man must avoid the danger. This duty he forgoes when he neglects the safer and the certain course of action, for the peril always remains in the thing itself, whatever be the opinion held on the matter. Suarez invoked for his argument the corroboration based on the distinction between the judgment bearing on law and on fact. The judgment bearing on law (*iudicium de iure*) connoted a relation to the one who acted. It completely removed the peril of sin, and stood as a cause sufficient for permitting one to follow a probable opinion, since the law had not adequately been made known, and since it was not in any way proper to burden man with doubtful obligations. The judgment bearing on fact (*iudicium de re*), on the other hand, indicated a relation to the factual object. It did not, however, remove the danger of damage or injury which was inherent in the fact itself. Hence there could not emerge a sufficient excuse for acting, because it was fairly evident that the danger was an intimate part of the fact itself and thus entailed the obligation of avoiding the emerging peril.[17] The examples which Suarez adduced in demonstration of the validity of his position are noteworthy: matters of faith, the sacraments, medicine, etc.[18]

However, from the preceding considerations, one must not conclude that Suarez wished to make of the principle *in dubiis tutior pars est sequenda* an iron-clad rule. He unquestionably simply wanted it to be the main key for the solution of a practical doubt of fact. Indeed, he expressly stated that when opinions simply imply a reference to facts themselves, man is frequently (*saepe*) obliged to prefer an almost certified opinion to a purely probable opinion, and the more probable opinion to the less probable one.[19]

[17] *De Bon. et Mal. Act. Hum.*, Disp. XII, sect. VI, n. 10.

[18] *De Bon. et Mal. Act. Hum.*, Disp. XII, sect. VI, nn. 8 & 10.

[19] *De Bon. et Mal. Act. Hum.*, Disp. XII, sect. VI, n. 10.

But, in a number of matters one could invoke particular principles in order to obtain the necessary practical certitude. Thus, an owner in good faith was not to be stripped of his lawful belongings on the strength of a doubt. The juridical rule, *in dubiis melior est conditio possidentis,* applied in his favor. Similarly the question of penalties could afford a derogation of the general principles. A crime had by proof to be established as certain both in law and in fact before a penalty could be imposed, since men were to be acknowledged, and therefore also adjudged, innocent until upon proof there was a disclosure of their guilt.[20] In short, it may be stated that Suarez held to the general rule, *in dubiis tutior pars est sequenda,* though he left room for exceptions in particular cases.

Suarez did not offer any treatment relative to the conversion of a doubt of fact into a doubt of law in his *De Bonitate et Malitia Actuum Humanorum.* However, it would be false to assume that he never envisaged this prospect. On the contrary, his treatise *De Legibus* studied the problem at some length. Indeed, in the sixth Book of this work, Suarez considered the possibility that the obligation of a law might cease in some particular instance even if the legislator had not removed the over-all obligatory character of the law. He engaged in a rather lengthy discussion of the various types of cessation of law. However, for the sake of brevity, it will suffice here to point out what he called a partial cessation. A partial cessation implied, first and above all, that the universal law was still in force, and that the legislator's will had not changed with respect to the obligation of the law, but simultaneously in the face of some extant fact that the law no longer obliged in that case.[21]

It was certain, Suarez stated, that the obligation of a law could cease in a particular instance, even if the comprehensive wording of the law seemed also to comprise this specific case, even if the case at hand did not stand as an exception to another law, and even if a dispensation had not been obtained. The fundamental reason which Suarez offered in support of this

[20] *De Bon. et Mal. Act. Hum.,* Disp. XII, sect. V, n. 8.

[21] *De Legibus,* Lib. VI, cap. VI, n. 1.

position he drew from the very nature of law itself. Law existed as a legal disposing of things in a universal manner. It was not possible for this universal arrangement of human law to be so correct in all particulars that at all times it remained proof against error. Indeed, human affairs under the organization of human laws continued subject to innumerable changes and contingencies. Thus it was utterly impracticable for a legislator to foresee all of them; but even granted that he could, he nonetheless could not make the proper provisions for them, because of the confusion that would result from the element of prolixity in the legislation. In short, universal law, to be just and reasonable, needed to be limited to what was the ordinary routine in human affairs. It was fitting, then, that the obligation of law cease in some particular instances, not because the law was abrogated, but because the legislator could not reasonably urge compliance with it.[22]

Suarez did not introduce any innovations in the treatment of doubt of fact. He followed the general principles of the jurists who preceded him. He did not institute any change of doctrine even in the matter of the conversion of a doubt of fact into a doubt of law, for on this point he declared himself a debtor of St. Thomas Aquinas and of the Thomistic school. While Suarez was indeed the great protagonist of probabilism, he evinced the status of a traditionalist in the field of doubt of fact.

[22] *De Legibus*, Lib. VI, cap. VI, n. 4; cap. VII, n. 11.

CHAPTER IV

DOUBT AS CONSIDERED BY SAINT ALPHONSUS

It seems strange, at first sight, to call upon St. Alphonsus, the Doctor of Moral Theology, in order to elaborate a point of jurisprudence. However, Moral Theology is very much concerned with law, divine and human, and with the primary effect of law, that is, the element of obligation. St. Alphonsus exercised a far-reaching influence in crystallizing the relations that exist between law and the obligations it engenders. There never arose in the minds of his predecessors any doubt that legislation implied the enactment of binding norms for the subjects of a legislator. Difficulties, however, sprang up when certain human laws, instead of serving as sure and reliable guide-posts for human conduct, did not provide clear-cut patterns of activity in all legal and moral issues.

Before the advent of St. Alphonsus, various theories had been offered in counteraction of the effects of doubtful laws. His great merit lies chiefly in the review that he made of the doctrines of his predecessors. He did not bring forward any novel principles, nor did he base them on a new argumentation. But through a wise selection of solid reasoning, he proved the value of the fundamental tenet of his moral system: a doubtful law does not bind.

It is the purpose of this chapter first to examine the doctrine of St. Alphonsus on doubt of law, and then to explore his teaching on doubt of fact.

Article 1. The Obligation of a Doubtful Law

The area wherein St. Alphonsus established the truth of the principle: a doubtful law does not bind, is his treatise *De Conscientia*. After a summary evaluation of the effect of doubt on the individual conscience, he undertook to investigate the rôle of opinion in the same domain.[1] He approved the position of

[1] S. Alphonsus de Ligorio, *Theologia Moralis*, Lib. I, nn. 20-89.

the preceding theologians in their acceptance of positive doubt and probable opinion as fairly synonymous, and readily used the two terms indiscriminately.[2] It might also prove pertinent to point out that he limited the basis of his analysis to the problem of two concurrent opinions which were equally probable, having expounded beforehand his principles relative to more probable opinions and to the need of moral certitude in ethical behavior.[3]

Positive doubt alone is here considered, and only such a doubt as cannot be speculatively resolved through the use of interpretation and of presumptions. The doctrine of St. Alphonsus, while it is clear, is somewhat involved. It was written at a time when controversies raged on moral issues. There are long lists of authorities whose testimony is offered in support of his contentions. Because of the nature of the present work, these will be omitted. The subject can be properly treated under two facets: the law in itself, and the law in man. The two aspects are often intertwined; nevertheless, for the sake of clarity, the writer proposes to examine them separately.

Law, if envisaged according to its intimate nature, cannot be doubtful and at the same time create an obligation. Indeed, St. Alphonsus categorically denied that a doubtful law can bind. He asserted that when an opinion which holds for man's liberty carries the same weight of probability as that which holds for the law, a grave doubt arises as to the very existence of the law. As a result, it can be said that the law has not been sufficiently promulgated and cannot therefore possess any obligatory character.[4]

The proof brought forth in substantiation of this statement rests on a twofold point of view: the intrinsic nature of law, and the need of promulgation for the creating of an obligation. In this respect it might be useful to indicate that St. Alphonsus

[2] *Opinio* denotat cognitionem dubiam aut probabilem alicujus veritatis. *Theologia Moralis*, Lib. I, n. 59.

[3] *Ibid.*, nn. 54 and 55.

[4] *Theologia Moralis*, Lib. I, n. 57.

made a wide use of St. Thomas Aquinas, whose texts served as a basis for the argumentation presented by St. Alphonsus.

Law, he stated, is a standard of human conduct. An indeterminate standard is inconceivable. What then could it measure? Of its very nature, a standard is set up to determine what is expected of all, and must necessarily be definite. So, too, must a law be definite; and an uncertain law cannot be a true law, and consequently cannot bind.[5]

St. Alphonsus laid significant stress on the need of promulgation as a means for the creating of an obligation. It is somewhat difficult to determine his usage of the term promulgation. In his argument he employed the word promulgation equivocally. With it he denoted at times, the knowledge of the law, and at times simply the authentic publication of the law.[6] It must be remembered, however, that the Saint was primarily a moralist, not a jurist; and the authorities he invoked in substantiation of his claim often furnished their doctrine equivocally. In this connection it should be realized that the principal source of his doctrine was St. Thomas Aquinas, who invariably made use of the terminology in the strict sense. The juridical promulgation of a law brought official knowledge of that law to the public at large, and for its net result, within the limits of what proved possible, it rendered each subject cognizant of the new legislation. Consequently, in practice, the stand adopted by St. Alphonsus is not reprehensible if properly understood.

There was a basic reasoning which constantly recurred in the unfolding of the moral system. Succinctly it stated: A law that is not adequately promulgated does not bind. But a doubtful law is not adequately promulgated. Hence it does not bind.[7] In order properly to assess the validity of the conclusion, one can surely gain further enlightenment by retracing the steps of the *Doctor Moralis*. The major premise was founded on the nature of positive law itself. Here St. Alphonsus maintained after St. Thomas Aquinas that human legislation is a regulation

[5] *Loc. cit.*

[6] *Theologia Moralis*, Lib. I, n. 58.

[7] *Ibid.*, n. 61.

set up in accordance with reason and promulgated by the head of the community for the common good.[8] A law which remained simply in the mind of the legislator was either an idle speculation or, at best, the cherished intention of setting up a law, but it was not a law that possessed a binding force.[9] Promulgation was essential to law in that it officially brought to the knowledge of the subjects the will of the lawmaker. Without this externalization, how could it be said that law is the standard of human conduct? A standard needs to be applied, and consequently must be known. St. Alphonsus advanced a step further. Not any kind of promulgation would suffice, he asserted, but only the one that was accompanied with certainty and clarity.[10] With this consideration he reverted to the necessity of clarity in law as a means for underlining the obligation which the law engenders: If promulgation was essential for a true law, it had also to share all the essential characteristics of law.

The minor premise, i.e., a doubtful law is not adequately promulgated, he substantiated in the following ingenious manner: " To bind, a law must of necessity be promulgated. However, if a doubtful law is promulgated, only a doubt, an opinion, or a problem as to the existence of a law is promulgated, and not a true law itself, for the elements of clarity and certainty are missing ".[11] St. Alphonsus remarked that for counteracting this argumentation it would be necessary either to hold that an unpromulgated law could bind, or that a doubtful law was really promulgated. Neither proposition, he added, could ever be proved.[12]

If a doubtful law is now examined from the point of view of the individual who is to be made subject to it, the same ubiquitous solution again emerges: a doubtful law entails no obliga-

[8] " Lex est ordinatio rationis ad bonum commune ab eo qui curam communitatis habet promulgata."—*Summa Theologica,* Ia IIae, q. 90, art. 4, in corp.

[9] *Theologia Moralis,* Lib. I, n. 57.

[10] *Ibid.,* n. 58.

[11] *Ibid.,* nn. 58, 61, 66, 67.

[12] *Ibid.,* n. 61.

tion. The proof advanced is again twofold: the first is based on the important rôle of knowledge; the second, on the primacy of human liberty with respect to law.

To establish the soundness of his stand, St. Alphonsus again appealed to a text of St. Thomas Aquinas, wherein the Angelic Doctor established an analogy between physical and legal bonds. The activity of a corporal agent on a given body was not of a compelling character unless there was a coercive contact between them. The same was true in legal matters. Indeed, the command of a ruler could not bind his subject unless the command reached and coerced the subject, and this could result exclusively through knowledge of the command. Hence, if the subject had, not a real knowledge of the law, but only an inkling or an opinion regarding it, the contact between the lawgiver and his subject was not coercive, and the law did not bind.[13] It must be remarked here that knowledge, i.e., *scientia*, was adverted to in the technical sense of the Schoolmen, for whom it meant a "*cognitio certa*."[14]

The position of St. Alphonsus relative to the primacy of human liberty in respect to law followed as a corollary from the preceding argumentation. Indeed, it was the core of his Moral System. When the probability that favored liberty was equal to that which favored the law, it was liberty that reaped whatever measure of favor the law could bestow. This was the basic consideration from which St. Alphonsus set out to erect his system. He accepted the truth of this premise, for when equal probability existed for the law and for liberty, the situation was the result simply of perplexity, and not of the presence of a true knowledge of the law.[15] Knowledge alone could lead to the emergence of an obligation. Liberty, of its very nature, stood as something antecedent to law. Consequently a doubtful law, in and of itself, could not induce an obligation certain in its existence and clear in its impact, or, to state the same truth in a form so dear to St. Alphonsus, an uncertain or doubtful obligation was not an obli-

[13] *Ibid.*, n. 73.

[14] *Ibid.*, n. 74.

[15] *Loc. cit.*

gation at all, because man's liberty evinced no restraint as long as it was not certainly and unmistakably affected by a bond of the law.[16]

St. Alphonsus went to great pains to elaborate his conclusion: *lex dubia non obligat*. He was continually harrassed by authors who in the history of theology have been all but forgotten. Nonetheless, they forced the *Doctor Moralis* to seek out all the possible proof which would foster an adequate basis for his position. That he achieved a large measure of success is clearly borne out by the Code of Canon Law.

Article 2. Law and Doubt of Fact

In order to assess accurately the teaching of St. Alphonsus on the doubt of fact, one must properly keep in mind a few relevant notions. Confusion could quite easily enter into an analysis of his work. This confusion could be partly occasioned by his terminology, and partly derived from an oversimplification of his ideas. In his treatise of a doubtful conscience, he asserted that a positive doubt usually is synonymous with a probable opinion.[17] He then distinguished doubt as speculative or as practical; no mention was made of the *dubium iuris* or the *dubium facti*. When he dealt with the element of probable opinion, a distinction was invoked between probability of law and probability of fact.[18] His definitions of a probable opinion of law and a practical doubt show that both are concerned with the lawfulness of an act, whereas a probable opinion of fact and speculative doubt relate to the actual nature of an action.[19]

In spite of such apparent similarities, it is imperative to keep the two divisions completely separate, because the principles and the consequences derived therefrom will not consistently dovetail. St. Alphonsus and the moral theologians of his era understood a practical doubt as one which has as its object the formal and intrinsic lawfulness of an action to be performed here

[16] *Theologia Moralis*, Lib. I, n. 26 and n. 74, in medio.

[17] *Theologia Moralis*, Lib. I, n. 20.

[18] *Ibid.*, n. 41.

[19] *Theologia Moralis*, Lib. I, n. 21 and n. 41.

and now, while a speculative doubt contemplated either an action in general or the objective truth of its material lawfulness.[20] Probability of law, on the other hand, concerned the existence, the sense and the extent of the law, and, in a wider sense, the existence and the extent of such instruments, e.g., a vow, a contract, as might bind an individual. In this respect it could be said to have as an objective the lawfulness of an act. Probability of fact emerged when the existence and the extent of a law were indeed certain, but when there was no certainty that in a particular case a concrete fact was invested with the conditions postulated as essential if the law was to become applicable.

From these notions St. Alphonsus construed the principles governing the morality of doubts of fact. The first reads thus: It is never permitted to make use of a *factually* probable opinion when there is danger of physical or moral harm to oneself or to another. This contention was most adequately supported in the very light of the nature of probability. Indeed, probability resulted from the subjective appraisal of the validity or the lawfulness of an action as based on a probable opinion. It implied some fear regarding the opposite view. If, however, an opinion was held to be probable when in reality it was erroneous, the action stemming therefrom was either invalid or unlawful, because validity and lawfulness were determined, not by a subjective judgment, but by objective norms of law. Thus, if saliva were employed as the material for a baptism, the latter would be invalid by the positive divine law, and no amount of probability to the contrary could ever derive a valid baptism from such a ceremony.[21]

From this principle St. Alphonsus deduced consequences relative to areas in which it was unlawful to use probable opinions of fact, because of the grave physical or moral harm which might be visited upon oneself or upon others. It was a matter of necessity always to follow the safer estimation, or that which proved morally certain in matters of faith and in all the means

20 Waffelaert, *De dubio solvendo in re morali,* p. 142.

21 *Theologia Moralis,* Lib. I, n. 42.

which were essential for the attaining of eternal salvation.[22] The same rule applied to the administration of the sacraments, to the prescription of medicine by doctors, to the dispensing of justice by a judge.[23] In short, it was never permitted to use a probable opinion of fact which might result in some injury or wrong to another or to oneself.[24] The opinion based on the probability of law was treated in an altogether different manner, as is evidenced in the preceding article.

In his treatment of a doubtful conscience, St. Alphonsus made it clear that one cannot act in line with what is suggested in consequence of a negative doubt, because the reasons which give rise to the opinion are so weak as to render the action unreasonable. However, when the opinion drew support from a serious motive, then really a positive doubt was encountered, and this latter doubt, as has been seen, was nearly always to be likened to probable opinion. Consequently, a positive doubt could reflect a *dubium iuris* or a *dubium facti*, and the principles studied above as relating to probability of law and probability of fact very aptly find their respective application here.

Speculative and practical doubt were also elaborated by St. Alphonsus. Speculative and practical doubt should indeed not be confused with doubt of law and doubt of fact, for each of them can point either to a doubt of law or to a doubt of fact. Indeed, a practical doubt envisages the morality or the legality of an action to be performed here and now. This doubt may well relate to the law itself, but it can also relate to the fact concerning which there is question, namely, whether it equates the postulated juridical conditions that make the law applicable in the case. The same holds true for a speculative doubt, which does not immediately pursue a course of action, but studies abstract considerations. In abstraction from the necessity of action, the contemplation of a law's existence or extent can very well lead to the emergence of a doubt of law. Again, with all necessity of action precluded, one could intellectually visualize

[22] *Ibid.*, n. 43.

[23] *Ibid.*, nn. 44, 47, 48.

[24] *Ibid.*, n. 52.

that a particular fact is only doubtfully encompassed within the scope of a law, and thus a speculative doubt could arise.

With this in mind, one may now proceed to enumerate the principles St. Alphonsus formulated. The first asserted that it is never permitted to act with a practically doubtful conscience; if one would nevertheless act, one would sin.[25] The reason upholding this sweeping rule stems from the premise that in acting with a practically doubtful conscience one is operating blindly and with no certitude whatever that one's conduct will be in harmony with the norms of morality and legality. St. Alphonsus required that before anyone could rightfully act he had to convert the doubt into a status of moral certitude through the use of reliable reflex principles.[26] The second principle allowed one to act when one labored under a speculative doubt, so long as moral certitude of the morality and lawfulness of the act could be obtained through the reflex principles. At this point St. Alphonsus referred to his Moral System, which furnished, as he felt, the necessary instruments for the achieving of a moral certitude.[27]

It is manifest that the two rules of action concerning doubt did not expressly distinguish between the *dubium iuris* and the *dubium facti.* This distinction, however, was necessarily to be maintained in the light of the Moral System. The doubt of law was not and could not be binding in either instance of the foregoing rules, because St. Alphonsus pointed to the use of the reflex principles: *lex dubia non obligat,* and *melior est conditio possidentis,* which were subsequently explained at length.[28]

What of the doubt of fact? St. Alphonsus clearly stated that one could not act when face to face with a practical doubt. Yet, when he adverted to the necessity of gaining moral certitude through the use of reflex principles, he did not distinguish between doubt of law and doubt of fact. The principles which he adduced dealt exclusively with the doubt of law; he invoked them in view of the conflict between equal probabilities for law

[25] *Ibid.,* n. 22.

[26] *Ibid.,* n. 24.

[27] *Ibid.,* n. 25.

[28] *Ibid.,* n. 26.

and liberty. Regarding the practical doubt of fact, one of two steps had to be taken: one had either entirely to refrain from acting, or one could act after attaining a favorable status through a use of the reflex principles. In the latter event, one could conceivably judge that the extent of the law which might govern the fact remained doubtful, and that in consequence the law did not oblige for lack of certified content. In other words, one had to be able to convert a doubt of fact into a doubt of law, if one wished to take effective action.

The problem was not quite so acute when a speculative doubt of fact was encountered. Immediacy of action was not a necessity, for the consideration of doubt remained rather abstract. Again St. Alphonsus required the possession of moral certitude as derived from reflex principles. Was this to be understood as an open invitation for the reduction of a doubt of fact to a doubt of law, or was it an indication that a dispensation should or needed to be obtained? This latter procedure afforded the moral certitude that the action could be undertaken licitly. However, St. Alphonsus never expressly stated that a doubt of fact could be converted into a doubt of law, and he left no inkling whatever regarding the advisability of a dispensation, even when he treated dispensation *ex professo*.[29]

Without any qualification of the justice due to St. Alphonsus, one may state that his treatment of the doubt of fact did not in itself afford much that was new. He upheld the condemnations of Innocent XI (1676-1689) relative to the use of probable opinions in matters of faith and the sacraments.[30] However, he seemed not completely clear in his elaboration of the doubt of fact, and this undoubtedly permitted succeeding generations to make use of his principles in such way as to bring about the present practice of converting a doubt of fact into a doubt of law as a solution for perplexing problems.

[29] *Theologia Moralis*, Lib. I, nn. 178-202.

[30] H. Denzinger, *Enchiridion Symbolorum* (quod a C. Bannwart denuo compositum iteratis curis edidit J. B. Umberg (26. ed., Friburgi Brisgoviae: Herder & Co., 1947), nn. 1151-1153.

PART II

COMMENTARY ON CANON 15

INTRODUCTION

LAW is an ordinance of reason for the common good, made by him who has care of the community, and then promulgated by him.[1] Its proper effect is to engender an obligation. However, it can readily occur that one may be freed from such a bond. The Code of Canon Law provides for this in numerous and diverse fashions. Indeed, by abrogation, derogation, contrary custom, a law may cease to affect the entire community. Yet, there are instances wherein the ecclesiastical legislator has provided that his law does not reach one or another of his subjects, even though the law has been duly constituted and promulgated, and even though the law has not been revoked.

Canon 15 explicitly deals with the case wherein the obligatory character of a law does not obtain in the face of doubt. With a view to a proper analysis of the legislation of the Church in this matter, doubt of law will first be considered, and in a subsequent chapter doubt of fact will be studied.

[1] [Lex est] ordinatio rationis ad bonum commune ab eo qui curam habet communitatis promulgata.—St. Thomas, *Summa Theologiae*, Ia IIae, q. 90, art. 4, in corp.

CHAPTER V

LEGES . . . IN DUBIO IURIS NON URGENT

This provision is an innovation in ecclesiastical legislation. The Church has incorporated in its legal system the practical conclusion of centuries of acrid debate in the field of jurisprudence and moral theology. However, as Van Hove (1872-1947) has pointed out, this canon does not propose to solve the problem of probabilism in the moral field.[2] As was shown in the historical section, the controversies relative to the doubtful conscience sought primarily to seek out a solution in the moral field. It was on this occasion that the speculative treatment of "*lex dubia non obligat*" came into being.

For a clear exposition of the juridical enactment relative to the doubt of law as found in the Code, the meaning of this principle will be appraised, and in a second article its application to the various areas of ecclesiastical legislation will be considered.

Article 1. The Meaning of the Principle: "*Leges . . . in dubio iuris non urgent*".

Section I. The Notion of Doubt in Canon 15

The proper understanding of the principle embodied in canon 15 is primarily premised on the concept of doubt. It was shown earlier that doubt is a state of the mind relative to adherence to truth. This state of the mind, while speculatively equivalent to the withholding of assent to truth, is nonetheless practically accepted by the theologians and canonists as the qualified acceptance of a proposition based on some probability. This gives rise to the various species of doubt. Doubt can be positive or negative, according to the presence or the absence of valid motives for doubting; it will be objective or subjective if the reasons for

[2] Hove, *Commentarium Lovaniense in Codicem Iuris Canonici*, Vol. I, Tom. II, *De Legibus Ecclesiasticis* (Mechliniae-Romae: Dessain, 1930), p. 233. This work will henceforth be cited as *De Leg. Eccl.*

the doubt depend on or abstract from reality; it will be vincible or invincible, if it can or cannot be resolved with the use of interpretations and of other juridical implementations.

Doubt, as envisaged in canon 15, must be positive. A positive doubt arises when there exist motives for doubting, whereas a negative doubt implies the absence of such motives. Negative doubt is essentially an unreasonable basis for human activity, for prudence requires that there be present some reason for doubting. Furthermore, negative doubt, if viewed practically, can be likened to ignorance, stemming as it does from grounds which of their nature do not suffice for the raising of a doubt.[3] The ecclesiastical legislator has positively determined by law in canon 16 what is to be done in the case of ignorance. Consequently, a negative doubt is not a true doubt, and cannot be understood as the type of doubt postulated in canonical legislation.

The nature of things demands further that the doubt be objective. Objective doubt specifies that the positive motives which are considered correspond to reality. It is distinguished from subjective doubt, which is gratuitously accepted by the intellect. Subjective doubt is essentially the preconception of a mind which lacks the proper knowledge or familiarity with a topic. A real doubt, of its very nature, requires that one evaluate the alternatives of a contradiction. This the subjective doubt fails to achieve, and hence it cannot be termed a true doubt.

It frequently occurs that doubts which are positive and objective in character will affect a law, and yet not fall within the scope envisaged by canon 15. Indeed, the application of the rules of interpretation and of the various devices, such as presumptions, furnished by the legislator will very often quickly dispel doubt. Such vincible doubts cannot be received within the framework of this study, because their acceptance would reduce to naught and contradict the positive enactments of the lawmaker. The very presence of the canons regarding interpretation postulates that a doubt be invincible before use can be made of canon 15. Invincible doubt is defined as one which can-

[3] " . . . propter defectum moventium."—*De Verit.*, q. 14, a. 1.

not be dispelled even after a diligent examination. This investigation necessarily requires the employing of all ordinary means for the obtaining of moral certitude relative to the contents of the law and the mind of the legislator. Should this fail, then and then alone will it be permissible to invoke the prescription of canon 15.

A positive, objective and invincible doubt can arise relative to the law itself, or relative to some particular fact. The former is a *dubium iuris*, while the latter is termed a *dubium facti*. Doubt of fact will be treated in a subsequent chapter.

SECTION II. THE LAW ENVISAGED IN CANON 15

The laws which can fall under a doubt of law must of necessity be ecclesiastical laws, that is, the body of laws enacted by the lawful ecclesiastical authority for the government of the Church. It cannot be too urgently stressed that the natural and the positive divine laws do not and cannot fall within the competence of canon 15, even if they should be embodied in the Code of Canon Law. This assumption can be established from several quarters.

Natural law, stated St. Thomas, is the participation of the eternal law in the rational creature.[4] It is essentially the divine command intimated to man by the light of reason relative to the exigencies of his rational nature. Natural law necessarily proceeds from God, the Supreme Lawmaker, and as such is beyond the competence of the human legislator.

Positive divine law is, in some respects, much like the natural law. God is its author. While it may contain precepts of the natural order, it was revealed by God and is directed to the attaining of the supernatural end of man. As a consequence, it cannot fall under the power of human legislation, and canon 15 cannot be applied to the positive divine law.

Furtherfore, the principle under study is contained in the Code under the title "*De legibus ecclesiasticis.*" Ecclesiastical law is human law, immediately deriving its origin from human legislators with authority in the Church. Titles are employed in the Code of Canon Law for the purpose of limiting the material embodied under them to a narrow field. It follows then that ec-

[4] *Summa Theologiae*, Ia, IIae, q. 91, a. 2.

clesiastical legislation must solely be concerned with human law, and that the principle under study must be confined to a strictly ecclesiastical area.

SECTION III. THE MEANING OF "*lex dubia non obligat*" AS CONTAINED IN THE CODE

The sense of the first portion of canon 15 thus becomes obvious. Whenever a doubt of law, based on the proper motives which truly exist in reality, and insoluble after a diligent application of interpretative norms, is discovered relative to some particular enactment, the ecclesiastical law does not bind. As was shown in a preceding chapter, a doubt of law concerns the existence, the signification, the extent or the cessation of a law. A positive and objective doubt, insoluble after an assiduous effort at interpretation and bearing on the existence, the sense, the comprehension or the cessation of a particular law, even if that law be invalidating or disqualifying, is a doubt of law, and, consequently, the particular law which is thus the subject of such a doubt is not of an obligatory character.

Indeed, if the existence, the sense or the extent of a law is truly doubtful, the incertitude springs from the fact that the law has not been sufficiently well promulgated, and, as a result, cannot be adequately known.[5] In this respect, St. Thomas stated: No one is bound to obey the command of a king or a ruler unless the order reach the one so commanded; it reaches him by virtue of knowledge. Hence no one is bound by a law unless he knows that law.[6]

While the great majority of the canonists are generally agreed that a true doubt concerning the existence, the sense and the extent of a law constitutes a doubt of law, there has arisen a controversy relative to the cessation of law as being included in the concept of legal doubt. This difference of opinion arises from the interpretation given to canons 6, n. 4, and 23. Canon 6, n. 4, reads: When it is doubtful whether a prescription of a canon

[5] Suarez, *De Bon. et Mal. Act. Human.*, Disp. XII, sect. V, n. 7.

[6] "Unde nec ex imperio alicuius regis vel domini ligatur aliquis, nisi imperium attingat ipsum cui imperatur; attingit autem ipsum per scientiam. Unde nullus ligatur per praeceptum aliquod nisi mediante scientia illius praecepti."—*De Verit.*, q. 17, a. 3.

disagrees with the old law, the latter must be upheld. It establishes the relation which must exist between the pre-Code legislation and the present codification when there is doubt concerning a discrepancy between old and new laws. Canon 23 states: In doubt, the revocation of an already existing law is not presumed, but recent laws must be adapted to older laws and, as far as possible, made to harmonize with them. This enactment is meant to regulate the relationship which must exist between the law of the Code and later laws when a doubtful disagreement arises between them.

According to some commentators, the presumption under which an older law enjoys its continued existence in the case of a true doubt is such that the older law yet prevails, and its cessation cannot fall under the prescription of canon 15. Hence, canon 15 cannot be employed, since the doubt has been practically and effectively reduced by the positive prescription of canon 23.[7] Indeed, according to Michiels, the legitimate application of canon 15 to a speculative doubt does not suffice. It is required that a doubt be speculatively and practically irreducible, that is, a doubt which persists after the use of interpretative and presumptive rules. So long as the presumption contained in canon 23 prevails, the speculative doubt concerning the revocation of a prior law must be considered as practically solved or eliminated by virtue of the reflex principle therein contained, and consequently there are no grounds for a legitimate application of canon 15.[8]

There is then only one manner of upholding the revocation of an older law: proof of its cessation.[9] However, if proof is ad-

[7] "In canone 15 directe de dubio circa legis *existentiam*; in canone 6 sub 4° directe de dubio circa Codicis *discrepantiam* cum jure praeexistente, in canone 23 directe de dubio circa legis praeexistentis *revocationem* agitur. Hinc *indirecte* solummodo in casibus canonis 6 et 23 dubium de legis existentia oritur, hoc vero dubium *praevenitur* et *practice* eliminatur, applicatis normis de dubia discrepantia vel revocatione in ipsis illis canonibus traditis, ita ut, sublato practice dubio, applicationi canonis 15 iam non detur locus."—Damen, "De vitanda iuris correctione ad normam Codicis," in *Apollinaris*, V (1932), 202.

[8] *Normae Generales*, I, p. 670, n. 3.

[9] "*Ratio juridica ultima* praesumptionis in favorem legis praeexistentis in canone statutae . . . haec est, quod factum, in casu *factum* revocationis . . . legis praeexistentis, non praesumendum est sed probandum."—Michiels, *Normae Generales*, I, 669.

duced, then there is no longer a doubt, but there is present instead at least a moral certitude, which obviates the use of canon 15.[10] Furthermore, because of the second clause contained in canon 23, this law enjoys not only a mere presumption, but also a true favor of law. Damen maintains that this favorable condition is founded on a triple presumption: namely, once a law has been enacted, it is presumed to be useful to the common good; the legislator will not easily revoke the law which he prepared with such care; finally, the community would experience more loss than utility from the change of a law, because it would disturb the accustomed order.[11]

Damen upholds the view that a prior law must not be reckoned as rescinded when doubt concerning the revocation is a strictly so-called doubt, that is, a doubt in the philosophical sense, wherein there are equal motives for affirming and again for denying, or when the judgment is suspended because of the presumption contained in canon 23. However, if notwithstanding this presumption, the arguments are such that a prudent and more probable opinion can be formed for the revocation of a law, the law may be held as revoked and it obligatory force ceases.[12]

The contrary opinion holds that the revocation of an older law cannot be presumed nor can it be deduced from conjectures. Nonetheless, the revocation of a prior law, after the prescribed efforts at reconciliation have failed, can be in doubt by reason of positive and objective arguments. Whenever such a true doubt arises, the principle of canon 15 can be applied.[13]

The writer accepts the latter position for the following motives. As Van Hove so succinctly stated it: since canon 15 does not distinguish, no distinction should be made between a doubt relative to the existence and extent of a law and a doubt regarding its cessation, as the aequiprobabilists would have it.[14]

[10] Michiels, *Normae Generales*, I, 670.

[11] "De vitanda iuris correctione ad normam Codicis," *Apollinaris*, V (1932), 203.

[12] Damen, "art. cit.," *Apollinaris*, V (1932), 59 et 201.

[13] Van Hove, *De Leg. Eccles.*, p. 236.

[14] *De Leg. Eccles.*, p. 236.

Then, Damen also admits the possibility of a revocation when a more probable opinion stands in favor of the revocation. However, in his study of this question, the noted author insists that the term doubt, as used in the Code, be accepted in the strict philosophical sense: a suspension of assent.[15] It was shown earlier that doubt cannot be narrowed to that limited meaning, because according to the rule of interpretation, as embodied in canon 18, a law must be interpreted in the light of the proper signification of its terms. The theologians and canonists have given to the word doubt a usual and proper sense: the acceptance of a proposition with some fear regarding its counterpart; and it is on this sense that the juridical and moral elaboration of the dictum "*lex dubia non obligat*" is premised. Hence, doubt as noted in canon 23 must have the same meaning as the doubt which receives mention in canon 15. Consequently, apart from all presumptions and conjectures that a law is revoked, if an objective and positive doubt should arise as to the revocation of an older law, the doubt is a doubt of law, and the older law is without obligatory force.

In the formation of a judgment relative to the revocation of a law, one is confronted with two arguments: one favoring the revocation, the other militating against the revocation and stressing the presumption for the non-modification of the law. If, in spite of this weighty presumption, solid reasoning should afford a serious basis for the probability of the revocation of the law, the revocation of the law is by no means presumed, and there still persists a law that is undeniably doubtful.[16]

Furthermore, if canons 23 and 6, n. 4, expressed the last word as regards the relations of new laws with the older legislation, canon 15 would of necessity be restricted simply to entirely new juridical enactments having no link with the past; such does not seem to have been the mind of the legislator, inasmuch as no positive indication of it can be found.

It is true that one must not proceed too hastily in declaring a prior law revoked when a doubt arises. Indeed, the legislator

[15] "De vitanda iuris correctione ad normam Codicis," *Apollinaris*, V (1932), 57, 58.

[16] Philippot, *De Dubio in Jure praesertim Canonico* (Brugis: Beyaert, 1947), p. 143.

has somewhat circumscribed the area wherein an older law may be considered doubtfully revoked. Canon 23 states that later laws are to be drawn to and, as far as it can be done, reconciled with the older laws. This section of the canon must be observed before a true doubt can be invoked. Nonetheless, when the reconciliation is attempted, how far must it be pressed before it can be regarded as successful or not? Canon 18 embodies the interpretative principles which govern the doctrinal meaning of a law. If, after all this apparatus has been put into operation, the positive and objective doubt should still remain insoluble, canon 15 can be applied.

The purpose of canon 23 is to prevent too hasty a departure from the older law. However, from the presence of the words "*trahendae sunt*" it cannot validly be argued that a reconciliation must necessarily be effected; on the contrary, the clause "*quantum fieri possit*" imposes a definite limit to the potential extent of reconciliation. The measure certainly must stop short of absurdity and unreasonableness: that is required by the nature of things, and it seems inconceivable that the legislator would enact a law to determine what is obvious. Hence "*quantum fieri possit*" cannot mean anything else but the use of correct interpretation for the purpose of achieving a reasonable reconciliation. If the texts of the older and more recent laws must be tortured, if exceptional meanings of words must be employed for the achieving of harmony, this is not true interpretation nor real reconciliation, but cavil and verbal virtuosity which have nothing to do with jurisprudence. It cannot therefore be held, as does Michiels, that a speculative doubt relative to revocation must be considered practically solved by reason of the reflex principle contained in canon 23.[17] Such a solution, while it undoubtedly affords a large measure of prudence for action, does not suffice in the strict speculative field, in which truth is the primary objective, and the juridical entities are studied in their intimate nature.

The notion of a doubt of law encompasses the existence, the sense, the extent and the permanence of a law. Whenever,

[17] *Normae Generales,* I, 670.

therefore, in an ecclesiastical law, these various particulars of the law are in doubt, the law lacks obligatory force.

Article 2. The Areas Wherein the Principle Obtains

It has been shown that a positive and objective doubt concerning the existence, the sense, the extent or the permanence of a law is properly termed a doubt of law. Canon 15 confirms the rule that laws which labor under such a doubt are bereft of their obligatory effect. It now remains to determine the application of this legal principle to the various enactments as found in the Code of Canon Law.

SECTION I. LAW

All ecclesiastical laws, proceeding as they do from legitimately constituted Church authority, necessarily engender an obligation. This cogent force is directly and essentially derived from the manifested will of the legislator.[18] While it is primarily and adequately the effect of every law, the obligation is not the sole result induced by legislation. Indeed, the legislator may will simply that his law have obligatory force; yet, he may add to his prescription a coercive element in order to insure that the scope of the law may be more securely fulfilled.[19] Hence, to evaluate properly the operation of the principle "*lex dubia non obligat*" one should consider first the laws which induce simply an obligation, and subsequently advert to the laws which beyond this obligation produce also other legal effects.

A. Preceptive and Prohibitory Laws

a. The concept

A law is preceptive when it ordains what must be done; it is prohibitory when it commands what must not be done. The distinction between the two is of minor importance here, because they do not possess any special efficacy beyond that which is commonly essential to all law, namely an obligation. They differ principally in their respective manners of producing the obli-

[18] *De Leg.*, Lib. III, cap. 20, n. 5.

[19] *De Leg.*, Lib. I, cap. 15, n. 16.

gation. Preceptive law will order that a positive act be done: if that act be omitted, the law will be violated. This act must necessarily be good or at least indifferent, else the law would command evil and would no longer be a valid law. From its inception as a law, preceptive law binds and continues to obligate so long as it remains a law. It does not, however, oblige at each moment, but only at the periods determined by the prescription. On the other hand, prohibitory law seeks to procure the omission of an act. As such, it consequently must forbid only evil acts. The violation of a prohibitory law results from the commission of the forbidden act. Because of the evil which it wishes to ward off, the prohibitory law will necessarily be operative at all moments throughout the time it exists as a binding norm.[20]

Preceptive and prohibitory laws produce the same effect: obligation; they differ solely in regard to the manner of inducing the obligation. Beyond the obligation, neither a preceptive nor a purely prohibitory law has any further legal effect.[21]

b. Comparison with the principle

Preceptive law urges that a person act in definite circumstances; prohibitory law forbids that certain actions be done. They both give rise to an obligation, but in diverse manners. In so far as they fall within the scope of canon 15, the difference in the mode of inducing the obligation is quite immaterial. The important factor lies in the obligation itself, since these laws have no specific efficacy beyond the moral and juridical bond which they engender. Hence they offer no special difficulty when a legal doubt arises.

If a doubt bears on the existence of a preceptive or prohibitory law, there must of necessity follow a similar doubt relative to its corresponding obligatory character. It is a principle of jurisprudence that law does not effectively bind unless it be adequately promulgated and disclosed to men. Promulgation is an essential property which gives existence to a law for the precise

[20] *De Leg.*, Lib. I, cap. 15, n. 4.

[21] It will later be shown that invalidating laws have some characteristics in common with prohibitory laws, but they cannot properly be termed simply prohibitory laws.

reason that it concretely brings to the community the expressed will of the legislator. The will of a legislator cannot be certainly known unless it be certainly manifested. Consequently when the existence of a law is doubtful, the obligation inherent in the law is not adequately shown, and the law cannot be termed a reasonable ordinance designed for the common good.

A doubtfully existing law cannot be a standard for human activity; the promulgation was at best defective. Defective promulgation is the equivalent of a lack of promulgation. If promulgation is essential for a true law, it must share all the essential characteristics of law.[22] Further, a true doubt relative to the existence of a law does not suffice to limit the natural scope of liberty. Indeed, man very definitely and surely possesses liberty, and until the legislator has positively and certainly curbed the use of that liberty with a preceptive or prohibitory law, freedom maintains its continued sway.[23]

It may be abundantly clear that a preceptive or prohibitory law exists, and yet some positive doubt may arise concerning the sense of that law. Such a doubt is truly a *dubium iuris,* centered as it is on the very law itself. Canon 15 definitely applies, and under those circumstances the law lacks binding force. The fundamental principle of jurisprudence which obtains in such a situation is the one proposed by St. Thomas: a person is not bound by a law unless he knows the law in question,[24] and a positive doubt cannot in any way be construed as knowledge. Law is a standard of human activity having cogent force. To effect an obligation, the law needs to be known. Even if the law be known to exist, it is not by this token that the law gains binding force; it is postulated further that its object be delimited and its signification be made manifest. Law, of its very nature, is the externalization of the legislator's will. The lawmaker seeks to obtain some specific purpose for the common welfare. It

[22] *De Leg.*, Lib. I, cap. 11, nn. 3 and 6; *De Bon. et Malit. Act. Hum.*, Disp. XII, sect. V, n. 7.

[23] *De Bon. et Malit. Act. Hum.*, Disp. XII, sect. V, n. 7.

[24] *De Verit.*, q. 17, a. 3.

would be unreasonable to assume that his subjects are bound by a doubtful tie.[25]

The case may readily be visualized when the existence and the signification of a preceptive or prohibitory law are certainly known, but a positive doubt may arise relative to the extent of this law. Thus, it would be clear that such a law would have force in determined instances, while at the same time it would be doubtful that other objects fell within the scope of the law. Such a situation is definitely within the realm of canon 15. It is in many ways analogous to that which obtains with reference to the sense of a law. Wherever the law surely applies, it is incontestable that an obligation must necessarily result. Yet, when a doubtful comprehension is encountered, an obligation in this particular field cannot be sustained, since the law does not clearly encompass such aspects and, consequently, the will of the legislator has not been adequately manifested in this respect.

Whenever the permanence of a preceptive or prohibitory law is questioned because a doubt has arisen relative to its continued existence, the problem is a *dubium iuris* and, as such, falls under the prescription of canon 15. The continued existence of a law which certainly existed can become doubtful in various ways. Indeed the legislator may revoke his law without duly advising his subjects, or else the purpose of the law may be such as to render it useless for the achievement of the common good, or again the prior law may have been doubtfully supplanted with more recent legislation which does not possess all the features of the older law. If a duly motivated and real doubt arises regarding the permanence of a law, the law must needs be considered doubtful, and it cannot induce an obligation. There is no question here of mere conjecture or of groundless discussion, but of a doubt which is consequent to objective reasons militating for and against the continued existence. Even the presumption that jurisprudence favors the permanence of a law does not irrevocably solidify the law's continued existence. A solid opinion will readily suffice to overcome the normal presumption for the law's permanence, because it is a prudent standard for human activity.

[25] *De Leg.*, Lib. VI, cap. 1, n. 11.

A doubt relative to the existence, the signification, the extent or the permanence of a preceptive or prohibitory law is a legal doubt. Whatever be the area touched by such a doubt, the obligation which is normally produced by that law ceases to obtain.

B. Invalidating and Disqualifying Laws

This survey into the field of "*leges irritantes et inhabilitantes*" does not have the pretension of exhausting the subject. The work has already been done.[26] Rather, the study proposes to prepare the way for the application of the principle "*lex dubia non obligat*" to invalidating laws. First the nature of this kind of law will be briefly studied, and subsequently the areas wherein canon 15 is applicable will be examined.

a. The Concept

An invalidating law (*lex irritans*) directly considers the act performed and denies it validity.[27] It does not consider the competence of persons to perform the act. Such an act, if envisaged from the point of view of the natural or the positive divine law, would be valid inasmuch as it would possess its natural constitutive elements.[28] If a law requires a certain form or prescribes definite formalities, all who wish to perform an act controlled by this law must conform the act to its prescription, else the act is invalid. Canon 1094 evinces such a law, as does canon 1530, § 1. Canon 1094 prescribes that a marriage is valid only when it is celebrated in a definite way.[29] Canon 1530, § 1,

26 Roelker, "The concept of invalidating laws," *The Jurist*, III (1943), 32-63; "The power to enact invalidating laws," *ibid.*, pp. 231-257; "The interpretation of invalidating laws," *ibid.*, pp. 364-403; "The effect and obligation of invalidating laws," *ibid.*, pp. 550-566.

27 Roelker, "The concept of invalidating laws," *The Jurist*, III (1943), 35; Michiels, *Normae Generales*, I, 320.

28 Van Hove, *De leg. eccles.*, n. 156, 157 and 160; Roelker, *ibid.*, p. 33. The contrary opinion is held by Michiels, *ibid.*, pp. 321-322, but the controversy has no bearing on the subject at hand.

29 *Ea tantum matrimonia valida sunt quae contrahuntur coram parocho, vel loci Ordinario, vel sacerdote ab alterutro delegato et duobus saltem testibus . . .*

n. 3, requires for a valid alienation that the permission of the legitimate superior be obtained.[30] The act itself is thus judged according to the prescriptions of the law.

A disqualifying law (*lex inhabilitans*) directly considers the person who performs or attempts to perform an act.[31] A disqualifying law denies legal competence to a person quite independently of physical capacity or moral readiness. Hence it is not primarily concerned with the act itself, but looks to the person. It will, however, ultimately deny validity to the act because of the legal incompetence attached to the person. Canon 1072 disqualifies clerics in major orders relative to marriage and rules any attempt to marry as an invalid act.[32] Thus invalidating law and disqualifying law differ according to the manner by which invalidity is determined. The net effect is the same: invalidity of the act performed. For this reason, the term invalidating law will be used in this study to mean both "*lex irritans*" and "*lex inhabilitans*", unless clarity require that the specific words be employed.

Prudence must be exercised in the evaluation of invalidating laws and their effects. Injustice can easily be perpetrated if a man's right to act is curbed, or the validity of an act is denied, without a clear and forthright declaration of incompetence and invalidity. In order to obviate this difficulty, the ecclesiastical legislator has positively stated in canon 11 the norms which establish the invalidating properties of a law. Invalidation or its equivalent must be expressed.[33] Difficulties, however, may be encountered when a law presents other legal facets. Thus an invalidating law may exhibit prohibitory and even penal characteristics.

A purely invalidating law simply denies any juridical effect to an act; it does not forbid a performance of the act. Such laws

[30] *Licentia legitimi Superioris, sine qua alienatio invalida est.*

[31] Roelker, *ibid.*, p. 36; Michiels, *op. cit.*, I, 320.

[32] *Invalide matrimonium attentant clerici in sacris ordinibus constituti.*

[33] *Irritantes aut inhabilitantes eae tantum leges habendae sunt, quibus aut actum esse nullum aut inhabilem esse personam expresse vel aequivalenter statuitur.*

are not of common occurrence in the Code of Canon Law. Examples of these laws can be found in canons 1017, § 1,[34] and 1513, § 2.[35] They are invariably expressed in positive terms. The legislator states how he wants an act to be performed, or under which conditions he will recognize the act. The juridical effect alone is contemplated.[36]

Very often, however, an invalidating law is expressed in negative words. The law then offers aspects which are prohibitory as well as invalidating. Such a law not only denies validity to an act, but it also forbids any performing of the act. It would be a serious mistake to confuse the effects proper to such laws. Their respective purposes make them two very distinct legal entities. A prohibitory law simply commands that an act must not be performed; an invalidating law nullifies the act or disqualifies the person. A prohibitory law sets up an obligation purely in conscience; on the other hand, an invalidating law, while it may oblige in conscience, goes beyond this and denies validity to the act. A prohibitory law, of its very nature, admits the excuse of ignorance or of moral incapacity and, on this basis, will frequently cease in its cogent force. Not so, an invalidating law. Invalidation is not premised on an obligation, but is derived from the will of the legislator who seeks to protect the common good of society and wishes to safeguard it more compellingly from fraud, injury and danger. The inviolable observance of invalidating laws is constantly urgent because their transgression presents a far graver danger to society itself.[37]

An invalidating law may also be a penal law. Indeed, the legislator may determine that an act is invalid or a person is disqualified and, beyond that, decree the addition of a penalty

[34] *Matrimonii promissio sive unilateralis, sive bilateralis seu sponsalitia, irrita est pro utroque foro, nisi facta fuerit per scripturam subsignatam a partibus et vel a parocho aut loci Ordinario, vel a duobus saltem testibus.*

[35] *In ultimis voluntatibus in bonum Ecclesiae serventur, si fieri possit, solemnitates iuris civilis; hae si omissae fuerint, heredes moneantur ut testatoris voluntatem adimpleant.*

[36] Michiels, *Normae Generales*, I, 323.

[37] Suarez, *De Leg.*, Lib. V, cap. 23, n. 6.

for the performance of the act. Such a case is envisaged in canon 2347. The alienation of Church property, when undertaken in violation of the rule expressed in canon 1530, § 1, n. 3, is branded with nullity unless the permission of the legitimate superior has been obtained. Besides the invalidity of the transaction, canon 2347 [38] establishes punishment for the perpetrator of this delict. Or else, the legislator may establish by law a penalty for certain specific crimes which will automatically produce definite disqualifying effects. Canon 2294, § 1,[39] offers an example of this. Yet, it must always be remembered that invalidity and penalties are separate juridical factors. Invalidity denies legal recognition to an act, while penalties provide punishment for violations of the law. One must study the law itself closely in order to determine whether invalidity or punishment is primarily sought, and the main points of interpretation are to be derived from the doctrine of the law which is primarily intended by the legislator.[40]

Thus, an invalidating law is not to be confused with a prohibitory law, nor may it be regarded as a penalty. An invalidating law may be prohibitory, and it may threaten punishment; but there are invalidating laws which neither set up a prohibition nor give promise of a reprisal. These distinctions are of capital importance when the efficacy of invalidating laws is studied.

[38] *Firma nullitate actus et obligatione, etiam per censuram urgenda, restituendi bona illegitime acquisita ac reparandi damna forte illata, qui bona ecclesiastica alienare praesumpserit aut in iis alienandis consensum praebere contra praescripta can. 534, § 1, et can. 1532*: There follows a list of the various punishments to be meted out in proportion to the value of the ecclesiastical goods with reference to which the violation was committed.

[39] *Qui infamia iuris laborat, non solum est irregularis ad normam can. 984, n. 5, sed insuper est inhabilis ad obtinenda beneficia, pensiones, officia et dignitates ecclesiasticas, ad actus legitimos ecclesiasticos perficiendos, ad exercitium iuris aut muneris ecclesiastici, et tandem arceri debet a ministerio in sacris functionibus exercendo.*

[40] Roelker, "The effect and obligation of invalidating laws," *The Jurist*, III (1943), 563.

b. Canon 15 and invalidating laws

Invalidating law is given specific mention in canon 15 for the sake of inclusiveness. The legislator could very well have excluded the words "*etiam irritantes et inhabilitantes*" from the text of his law, and yet, despite this exclusion, good jurisprudence would still require that invalidating laws fall under the regulatory prescription dealing with legal doubt. Indeed, canon 15 is contained under the title which treats of ecclesiastical laws. This selfsame title explicitly brings invalidating laws into focus in canon 11, and there is no evidence which would permit one to exclude these laws from the doctrine regarding the *dubium iuris*.

Invalidating laws, however, evince an individuality which is not generally found in preceptive and prohibitory laws. While the latter laws necessarily produce a moral and a juridical obligation, but are also strictly limited to that effect, the same cannot be said of invalidating law. It can be very broadly stated that two effects arise out of invalidating law as such: invalidity and obligation.[41] Yet, due care must be exercised lest the efficacy of invalidating laws be misinterpreted, for fundamentally an invalidating law achieves only what the legislator wills.

When the legislator enacts an invalidating law, he must necessarily intend that invalidity will brand every act that is contrary to this law. In so far as the subject at hand is concerned, it is rather immaterial whether the invalidity be brought about by the law itself or whether the law require a declaration of invalidity. These factors revolve about the time when an invalidating law will produce its effect, whereas the present study is concerned with invalidating law itself and its efficacy in the case of doubt.[42]

An invalidating law which without the intervention of a judge clearly specifies invalidity for an act contrary to it immediately produces its effect in both the internal and the external forum.

[41] Van Hove, *De Leg. Eccl.*, n. 159; Michiels, *Normae Generales*, I, 323; Wernz-Vidal, *Ius Canonicum*, Tomus I, *Normae Generales* (2. ed., Romae: Apud Aedes Universitatis Gregorianae, 1952), p. 212.

[42] For a study of the question when invalidating law takes effect, cf. Roelker, "The effect and obligation of invalidating laws," *The Jurist*, III (1943), 550-560.

If an invalidating law sets up the need of a judicial declaration or condemnation, invalidity is not effected in either forum until the sentence is pronounced. Hence, acts performed in contravention of such invalidating laws must be considered valid until the court has judged otherwise.[43]

The second effect which arises out of an invalidating law is the emergence of an obligation. It cannot be stated that the emergence of an obligation is a universal result of invalidating law.[44] Here again the will of the legislator will need to be closely examined. It is true that the legislator expects his law to be obeyed, but the precise point at issue is whether he has determined that his invalidating law engenders also an obligation in conscience.

It was previously shown that canonists conveniently distinguish between invalidating laws: some laws do no more than invalidate the act or disqualify the person; others forbid also the act which they invalidate; and, finally, the laws of either of these two categories may evince, in addition, some penal character.

An obligation in conscience is not innate to a law which simply invalidates the act or disqualifies the person.[45] The legislator has not signified his will to bind the conscience; he is content with simply manifesting the fact that one has to accept invalidity as the effect of the violation of such a law. In a word, the legislator has simply stated that, if an act is not performed according to the prescribed formalities, it is bereft of juridical effect. Thus the prescription of canon 1017, § 1, does not oblige in conscience as a command to be executed, but simply points out the conditions to be fulfilled if a valid betrothal is to be achieved.

43 Michiels, *op. cit.*, I, 327-331; Roelker, "art. cit.," *The Jurist*, III (1943), 560.

44 Suarez, *De Leg.*, Lib. V, cap. 20, nn. 5-7; Van Hove, *op. cit.*, n. 163; Michiels, *op. cit.*, I, 323; Roelker, *ibid.*, p. 561.

45 Suarez, *De Leg.*, Lib. V, cap. 20, n. 11; Van Hove, *De Leg. Eccl.*, p. 170; Michiels, *Normae Generales*, I, 323; Roelker, "The effect and obligation of invalidating laws," *The Jurist*, III (1943), 562.

When an invalidating law forbids also the act it invalidates, then the moral obligation resulting therefrom in no way differs from that of a purely prohibitory law. A prohibitory law always obliges one in conscience to omit an act. The presence of an invalidating clause has nothing to do with the necessity of omitting the act. It simply means that the legislator has strengthened his prohibition of the act. There follows a consequence of a more pronounced gravity for acting contrary to the will of the legislator. The element of invalidity when added to the element of prohibitition no more impedes the moral effect attaching to the act than the adjunct of a penalty in the case of penal law removes one's obligation in conscience to obey.[46]

An invalidating law may also be a penal law, that is, the legislator, beyond his will to prohibit and invalidate an act, may add a penalty to prevent violations. If in an invalidating law it is the penal aspect that is primarily intended, then the jurisprudence regarding penalties obtains. This will be considered in a subsequent section. If invalidity is the primary effect desired, then the doctrine regarding invalidating laws prevails, namely, there arises an obligation in conscience to forego the act because it is forbidden by the legislator. This prohibition is premised on the threat of punishment, which would be inconceivable if the act were not prohibited.[47]

It now remains to determine the rôle which a *dubium iuris* plays within the area of an invalidating law. Canon 15 states that in a legal doubt ecclesiastical laws do not exert any obligatory force. Legal doubt is the qualified assent given to a proposition relative to the existence, the sense, the comprehension, or the permanence of a law, but accompanied with some fear regarding an opposite proposition. If there is a positive doubt as regards the existence or the permanence of an invalidating law, jurisprudence requires, as it does for other species of laws, that the law be considered as non-existent. Consequently, the law cannot induce its invalidating effect. If the sense or the

[46] Suarez, *De Leg.*, Lib. V, cap. 20, n. 9; Van Hove, *op. cit.*, p. 171; Roelker, "art. cit.," *The Jurist*, III (1943), 561.

[47] Roelker, *ibid.*, p. 564.

extent of an invalidating law is doubtful, the invalidity of an act or the disqualification of a person cannot be asserted. While it is true that man does not possess all rights in society, his incompetence to act must in all justice be clearly and unmistakably evident, as must be certain and readily perceptible also the invalidity which will annul his act. Otherwise, law would no longer be an ordination of reason for the common good, but rather an item of arbitrariness and unreasonableness which would adversely affect the purpose of society.

There are invalidating laws which command the presence of certain formalities for the validity of an act.[48] Among these formalities, some may be considered legally substantial and others merely accidental or accessory to the observance of the law. For the validity of the act, all substantial formalities must needs be present. It is conceivable that a doubt of law could arise regarding the legally substantial character of one of the prescribed formalities and, as a result, this prescription would remain unfulfilled. Nonetheless, the act must be accepted as valid, since it is not clear that the legislator imposed the execution of this prescribed condition for the validity of the act.

On the other hand, a *dubium iuris* can be viewed from the aspect of one's obligation in conscience. In this regard, a purely invalidating law would not fall within the purview of canon 15, as it does not of itself produce an obligation in conscience to omit the act. Only a subsidiary and accidental obligation can be derived from it, namely, the necessity of protecting the rights of others. If the will of the legislator should be doubtful relative to this secondary effect of a purely invalidating law, then likewise the obligation in conscience resulting therefrom would necessarily be of a dubious character and consequently could not exercise any claim.

With respect to prohibitory invalidating laws, a legal doubt will operate as for a prohibitory law and, as a result, an obligation will not ensue. However, it is definitely possible that a *dubium iuris* may arise relative to one facet of a prohibitory invalidating law and not affect the other aspect. In such an oc-

[48] Canons 1017, § 1, and 1513, § 2, fall into this category.

currence, the prohibitory factor would be unmistakably clear while the invalidating clause would be legally doubtful, or vice versa. How, then, would the principle "*lex dubia non obligat*" apply? Should the entire law lose its efficacy, or should some effort be made for the salvaging of one or the other portion of the legislation? It is here asserted that the prohibitory area of the law which is clear and certain must yet possess some efficacy. It is undoubtedly true that a doubt concerning the existence or the permanence of such a law could not but affect the entire law itself and, as such, the law would be denied any effect, be it the inducing of an invalidity or the urging of an obligation in conscience. The scope within which such a possibility could arise is clearly the sense or the extent of the law. If the invalidating clause were doubtful and the prohibition certain, it is incontestable that invalidation could not follow, but that the obligation of omitting the act would unquestionably bind one in conscience. In a word, the law would not possess any invalidating character, yet nonetheless it would remain a prohibitory law and produce the effect proper to such a law. On the other hand, if the prohibitory aspect were legally doubtful, it is not likely that the invalidating clause could be certain. Indeed, in a prohibitory invalidating law, the legislator has determined the inevitable effect of invalidity as his reason for strengthening his precept to omit the act.

If compared with a penal law, the character of an invalidating law will quite readily emerge. Its purpose is to protect the common good, to see to it that acts are so produced that their uniformity will promote the good order of society. A penalty, however, has the purpose of punishing transgressions against preceptive or prohibitory laws. Invalidation, as a rule, is not added above and beyond the prohibition in a separate text, and this rule obtains for the great majority of penalties which are enacted in Book V of the Code of Canon Law. The notion of invalidation is included within the very words of the law itself, and the invalidity forms a unit with the prohibition in prohibitory invalidating laws; it is substantially one with the prohibition. It is not so with the penal law, where, as Suarez stated it, the unity or the plurality of the laws is an accidental item.[49] From that it may be deduced that, if the prohibition be doubtful, it does not bind, and consequently one is not held to a penalty which presupposes a delict. There is nothing here of the nature of a delict, because the morally imputable violation of a law is absent, since by virtue of the doubt the law does not exist. If the penal law is doubtful, one is not bound to observe the penalty, because an obscure or uncertain law is not a fit measure to assure uniformity of action in a community, and does not clearly indicate the legislator's will.

As can be seen, a penal law is a legal unit which applies after another legal unit, either preceptive, prohibitory, or prohibitory-invalidating, has been violated. But prohibitory-invalidating law is one unit which does not too readily admit of division. Invalidation does not of itself produce an obligation in conscience as regards the omission or the commission of an act. It necessarily follows, then, that if the prohibitory aspect of a prohibitory-invalidating law is doubtful, the law is incapable of effectuating a prohibition, and cannot have any invalidating effect.

Thus, an invalidating law operates in a fashion which is quite similar to that of other ecclesiastical laws in the face of a *dubium iuris.* It is when doubt affects only the invalidating aspect of a prohibitory-invalidating law that the prohibition may conceivably still carry on obligation in conscience.

SECTION II. PENALTIES

The efficacy of preceptive, prohibitory and invalidating laws in the face of legal doubt has been studied. There now remains the task to consider the rôle which a *dubium iuris* will play when it applies to penal legislation. It is not the intention of the writer to review the entire doctrine of penalties as it is incorporated in the Code of Canon Law. This would lead one unduly far afield, and would offer little of value for the question at hand. Rather, a succinct explanation of the concept of penal law will be offered, to be followed by an analysis of the efficacy of

[49] *De Leg.*, Lib. V, cap. 3, n. 2.

penalties and, finally, by a consideration of the relations between a legal doubt and penalties.

A. The concept

Penal law, in its basic acceptation, is that which decrees a penalty. It would be entirely irrelevant at this juncture to participate in the controversy relative to purely penal laws, as these certainly have no place in the Code of Canon Law. Canons 2215 [50] and 2195, § 1,[51] made it abundantly clear that the universal penal legislation of the Church is premised on moral guilt arising from the violation of a law to which a punishment has been added. Hence, it can be broadly stated that penal law contains two elements, one of which will command or forbid an act, and the other of which will enjoin a penalty against the transgressors of such a law.[52]

The concept of penal law becomes clear if its purpose is adequately appraised. The Church is a juridically perfect society, and as such necessarily has a social order which must needs be preserved. Any disturbance of this uniformity of conduct tends to obstruct the attainment of the end for which it was established. This disorder principally follows from the commission of delicts. Delicts, of their very nature, imply the morally imputable transgression of a law which is susceptible of punishment. Thus, penal law provides a juridical and punitive reaction by legitimate authority against those who contravene the finality of the Church.[53] Consequently the primary and essential purpose of the penalties provided by penal law is the punishment of crime for the restoration of public order.

[50] Poena ecclesiastica est privatio alicuius boni ad delinquentis correctionem et delicti punitionem a legitima auctoritate inflicta.

[51] Nomina delicti, iure ecclesiastico, intelligitur externa et moraliter imputabilis legis violatio cui addita sit sanctio canonica saltem indeterminata.

[52] Suarez, *De Leg.*, Lib. V, cap. 3, n. 1.

[53] Ottaviani, *Institutiones Iuris Publici Ecclesiastici*, I (3. ed., Typis Polyglottis Vaticanis, 1937), p. 311, ss.; Wernz-Vidal, *Ius Canonicum*, Tomus VII, *Ius Poenale Ecclesiasticum* (2. ed., Romae: Apud Aedes Universitatis Gregorianae, 1951), pp. 180-181.

However, this must not be understood in such wise as to preclude the possibility of other ends. The correction of the delinquent and the deterrence of the faithful from the commission of delicts are also envisaged, but these are extrinsic purposes and cannot necessarily and always be obtained. This twofold finality of penalties emerges from the consideration of canons 2215 and 2216. Canon 2215 provides for the correction of the delinquent and the punishment of the delict. On the other hand, canon 2216 enumerates the various species of penalties, thereby demonstrating the dual purpose of penal legislation.[54]

Penal law, in the Code of Canon Law, can be understood as that legislation which commands the performance or the omission of an act under the threat of punishment for its violation. In so far as it commands or forbids an act, it has the characteristics of a preceptive or a prohibitory law. The provision for a penalty clearly makes it a penal law. Yet, the legislator may even go further in his enactment of a penal law. He may so construct his legislation that the law will also disqualify the violator and invalidate his subsequent acts. In this respect, disqualification and the invalidity of the subsequent acts of a disqualified person will directly obtain for the preservation of the common welfare of society. The fact that a penalty is enjoined for the reinforcement of a preceptive or a prohibitory law directly connotes that the performance of an act forbidden by law, or the omission of an act commanded by law, is a delict, and as such is deserving of punishment. From this consideration it must not be implied that penal law is not directed to the attaining of the common good. Such an inference would deny that penal law can be properly classified as law, since it is essential for law to be enacted for the common good.[55]

[54] *In Ecclesia delinquentes plectuntur*:

1. *Poenis medicinalibus seu censuris.*
2. *Poenis vindicativis.*
3. *Remediis poenalibus et poenitentiis.*

[55] *Lex est ordinatio rationis ad bonum commune ab eo qui curam habet communitatis promulgata.*—St. Thomas, *Summa Theologiae*, Ia IIae, q. 90, art. 4, in corp.

It simply means that both disqualifying and penal laws will be enacted for the purpose of effecting the common good, but in diverse manners. While penal laws are essentially ordained for the punishment of delicts and secondarily for the correction of the delinquent and the deterring of the faithful from delicts, disqualifying laws are immediately concerned with juridical incompetence. Disqualification directly considers the person who performs the act, and ultimately denies validity to the act itself. Disqualification, of its very nature, is not the result of punitive legislation, but rather the consequence of a positive act of the legislator who has deemed it essential for the common good that a person be denied competence in certain matters. Certainly such enactments as the ones contained in canons 504, 1072 and 1439, § 2, are not punitive in character; they are a means of insuring the orderly functioning of society. Even when disqualification is added to penal law, as is the case in canons 2294, § 1, and 2347, n. 2, one must not lose sight of its true purpose. While in such instances it might appear to be a second penalty, in reality disqualification does not look to punishing the delict as such, but, beyond the penalty, it declares a person incompetent to act, in order to protect the very fiber of society itself.

A certain number of penal disqualifying laws can be found in the Code of Canon Law.[56] Penal invalidating laws can be considered under the twofold aspect of penalty and invalidation. At times the penal factor will predominate over the invalidating aspect, or again the contrary situation can possibly obtain. However, the ecclesiastical penal disqualifying laws are for the most part contained in Book V of the Code, and this fact seems to support the contention that in penal disqualifying laws the penal element is primary and the disqualification is secondary. Indeed, the penalty and the disqualification follow upon the violation of a law which is punishable in consequence of a penal disqualifying law. This delict is punished in consequence of the penal aspect of the law, and the disqualification immediately

[56] Cf. canons 2291, n. 9; 2294, § 1; 2298, n. 5; 2345; 2346; 2368, § 1; 2390, § 2; 2394, § 1; 2395; 2413, § 1.

sets in, since the accessory naturally follows the principal. Hence, in dealing with penal laws, one must exercise care lest one lose sight of the intention of the legislator in enacting his law.

B. The efficacy of penal law

Before setting out to determine the efficacy of penal law, the writer wishes to recall that the consideration of purely penal law has been excluded from this study. A discussion of the relative merits of the opinions favorable or opposed to purely penal law would uselessly burden the topic. Hence, the subject will be confined to the so-called mixed penalties, that is, to penal laws whose effects are simultaneously moral and penal.

As a general rule, penal law, precisely considered from the penal aspect, has the essential property of inducing a moral and juridical obligation. For the purpose of establishing the validity of this proposition, an anlysis of its component parts will clarify matters. Penal law is a true law. The simple addition of a punitive factor does not cancel out the essential characteristics of law. On the contrary, the added penalty places in bolder relief and reinforces the precept or the prohibition of the legislator. When the law orders or forbids an act, it clearly indicates the intention of the lawmaker to oblige one in conscience to perform or to omit this act. Hence, it follows that penal law produces a moral obligation.[57]

Then, too, delicts may disturb the good order of society. Penalties are foreseen in the law for the punishment of such delicts, and they are primarily ordained for the preservation of the social order.[58] Hence, a juridical relation obtains between the social authority and the perpetrator of such violations. This relation serves as the basis for the infliction of penalties on the guilty by the authorities, whose duty it is to preserve the society. The power to inflict punishment necessarily postulates the acceptance of the punishment by the guilty. This is termed

[57] Suarez, *De Leg.*, Lib. V, cap. 3, n. 8.

[58] Ottaviani, *Institutiones Iuris Publici Ecclesiastici*, I, 311.

a juridical obligation. But a juridical obligation which is proper to a penal law necessarily underscores a moral obligation for the subject to observe the penalty. Thus it can be said that penal law principally obliges one in conscience to perform or to omit a determined act, and, in the event that the law is contravened, to accept the penalty provided by the law.[59]

However, while this general principle is readily accepted, there now arises the problem as to when this obligation obtains. This will be greatly influenced by the type of penalty enacted in the law. Ecclesiastical penal laws are so divided that a violation of them entails either *latae sententiae* or *ferendae sententiae* penalties.[60] This distinction can perhaps be better understood if the difference of operation is closely observed. Certain penalties postulate the agency of a third party who will command their execution, while others are immediately operative by reason of the law itself. The former are termed *ferendae sententiae* penalties, the latter, *latae sententiae* penalties. In *ferendae sententiae* penalties, the law does not apply the penalty itself, but it does oblige one in conscience to carry out the penalty enjoined by the law once it is imposed by a judge. In *ipso facto* incurred or *latae sententiae* penalties, not only does the law produce the penalty, but it also obliges one in conscience to act in accordance with the punitive effect of the law.[61] Therefore, the obligation in conscience will vary in its inception according to the manner in which the penalty is incurred.

Whenever a penalty, as enacted in the law itself, does not require a sentence of any kind, it binds one in conscience from the very moment that the action punishable with such a penalty is performed. This obligation in conscience is concerned not only with the performance or the omission of an act as commanded by the law, but also with the acceptance of the penalty enacted for the violation of the law. Such is the traditional teaching of

[59] Suarez, *De Leg.*, Lib. V, cap. 3, n. 12; Michiels, *Normae Generales*, I, 305-307.

[60] Canon 2217, § 1, n. 2.

[61] Suarez, *De Leg.*, Lib. V, cap. 7, nn. 1, 2 and 5.

ecclesiastical jurists,[62] and it has been made a part of ecclesiastical law.[63]

However, instances arise when an *ipso facto* incurred penalty cannot be executed without the intervention of a third party, for instance a judge. In such a case, while the law prescribes a penalty for the delict, there may be reasons why one is not immediately obliged in conscience to observe the penalty. A declaratory sentence may have to be pronounced by the judge after the guilt has been established in order that the public observance of the penalty may be urged. There is not implied any present condemnation of the perpetrator of the delict, but simply a declaration by the judge that the penalty was *ipso facto* incurred at some earlier time. The obligation in conscience publicly to observe the penalty reaches its full force only when the judge declares that the penalty has been incurred.[64]

Jurisprudence has accepted the rule that no person is required to expose himself to the loss of his reputation. These considerations are incorporated in ecclesiastical law in canon 2232, § 1.[65] Yet the declaratory sentence evinces the penalty as retroactive to the time of the commission of the delict with the juridical effects foreseen by the law[66] and with the consequent obligation in conscience to carry out these effects.

The Code of Canon Law also envisages penalties which will be applied by means of a condemnatory sentence. Whenever a law enacts a *ferendae sententiae* penalty, the violator of this law

62 Suarez, *De Leg.*, Lib. V, cap. 5, n. 15, and cap. 8, n. 2; Reiffenstuel, *Jus Canonicum Universum* (5 vols. in 7, Parisiis: L. Vivès, 1864-1870), Lib. I, Tit. II, cap. 10, n. 226.

63 Canon 2232, § 1.—*Poenae latae sententiae . . . delinquentem, qui delicti sibi sit conscius, ipso facto in utroque foro tenet; . . .*

64 Suarez, *De Leg.*, Lib. V, cap. 8, n. 3; Reiffenstuel, *op. cit.*, Lib. I, Tit. II, cap. 10, nn. 227-228.

65 *. . . ante sententiam tamen declaratoriam a poena observanda delinquens excursatur quoties eam servare sine infamia nequit, et in foro externo ab eo eiusdem poenae observantiam exigere nemo potest, nisi delictum sit notorium . . .*

66 Canon 2232, § 2.—*Sententia declaratoria poenam ad momentum commissi delicti retrotrahit.*

is not bound in conscience to observe the enacted penalty until he has been condemned with a sentence from a judge. The condemnatory sentence is distinguished from the declaratory sentence in that the judge in the former instance inflicts the penalty, whereas in the latter case the judge simply declares that the enacted penalty has been incurred. Then, too, the obligation in conscience to observe the penalty and its related effects obtains from the moment of the condemnation in *ferendae sententiae* penalties. On the other hand, the declaratory sentence evinces the penalty and its effects as retroactive to the time when the delict was committed.[67]

Penal disqualifying laws operate in a manner which is substantially similar to that of ordinary penal laws. As a result, disqualification can be incurred *ipso facto* or it can ensue upon a condemnatory sentence. The Code of Canon Law offers examples of *ipso facto* sustained disqualifications: canon 2294, § 1, with reference to anyone branded with legal infamy, establishes some immediate disqualifications and enumerates the effects attached thereto.[68]

However, the condemnatory disqualification is more common than the one that is incurred *ipso facto.* In some instances the delict may be punished with an *ipso facto* incurred penalty, and the disqualification may ensue only upon a condemnatory sentence relative to the same delict.[69] In other cases the penalty and the disqualification will both obtain only after the condemnatory sentence.[70] Finally, a disqualification may be incurred *ipso facto,* and the penalty may ensue only upon a condemnatory sentence.[71]

67 Reiffenstuel, *Jus Canonicum Universum,* Lib. I, Tit. II, cap. 10, n. 231.

68 *Qui infamia iuris laborat . . . est inhabilis ad obtinenda beneficia, pensiones, officia et dignitates ecclesiasticas, ad actus ecclesiasticos perficiendos, ad exercitium iuris aut muneris ecclesiastici, et tandem arceri debet a ministerio in sacris functionibus exercendo.*

69 Canons 2345 and 2346 are examples of this mode of operation.

70 Canon 2368, § 1, gives evidence of this mode.

71 Such is the case in canons 2394, § 1; 2395 and 2413, § 1.

The extent of the disqualification must be indicated in the law, and the person guilty of violations which are punishable with a penal disqualifying law is obliged in conscience to observe the penalty and the disqualification. The time at which this obligation begins to bind will depend on the manner in which the disqualification was sustained.

C. *Penalties and the dubium iuris*

Penalties may reflect the presence of a legal doubt in divers manners. Punitive legislation necessarily presupposes that the legislator intended to strengthen his command or his prohibition regarding the performance of some act. However, this must not be construed in such a way that the penal enactment will necessarily contain within itself the command or the prohibition of the legislator. Very often, in the Code of Canon Law, the preceptive or prohibitory law and the penal law are materially separated.[72]

Thus, two possibilities of legal doubt can arise. Indeed, the preceptive or the prohibitory law can be legally doubtful, or the penal law itself can be affected with a *dubium iuris.* If the command or the prohibition of the legislator is legally doubtful, the very essence of the preceptive or prohibitory law is defective, and consequently the legislator has not enacted a true law. There cannot arise any moral obligation to obey what has only the appearance of law. As a result, the penalty enacted in punishment of the violations of such a doubtful, and as such inexistent, law is inane, since a moral obligation and the element of imputability cannot arise when there is no formal law.

However, the preceptive or the prohibitory law may be perfectly free of any legal doubt, but the penal law itself may be affected with a *dubium iuris.* Here the efficacy of the law is attacked in a different manner. The moral obligation engendered by the preceptive or the prohibitory law is not in the least impaired. There exists a full necessity in conscience to perform or

[72] Canon 166 contains a prohibitory law the violation of which is punishable in accord with the enactment contained in canon 2390. The same relation exists between canon 1530 and canon 2347.

to omit the act according to the prescription of the legislator. Nonetheless, when the law is legally doubtful, the penalty which was enacted by the lawmaker in punishment of the violations of his command or prohibition cannot be considered as punitive legislation. Legal doubt has bereft it of its true juridical character, and as a consequence the legally doubtful penalty is stripped of all obligation in conscience. Thus, one would be bound in conscience to obey the preceptive or the prohibitory law. Yet, if such a law were violated, the legal doubt concerning the penal character of the law would remove all obligation of submitting to the penalty.

For certain species of delicts, it sometimes happens that the legislator, beyond the ordinary penalties, also invokes a disqualification as a deterrent to the violation of his law.[73] Here again, if the *dubium iuris* centered about the command or the prohibition, the preceptive or prohibitory law would not engender a moral obligation. As a result, the penalty and the disqualification would not obtain, because of the absence of a delict. However, if the penal disqualifying statute itself is affected with a legal doubt, it does not seem possible that a disjunction of penalty and disqualification could be envisaged. Indeed, the enactment of penal disqualifying laws is justified for the purpose of punishing particularly odious crimes. The Church has ever been solicitous of graduating penalties according to the nature and gravity of the crime. A penal disqualifying law provides very serious punishment because, beyond the penalty, it deprives one of the competence to act. Because of this, a penal disqualifying law must be considered as a substantial unit of punishment. As a result, if a *dubium iuris* affected either the penalty or the disqualification, the entire law would be legally doubtful, and thus could not engender any obligation.

[73] Thus the violation of canon 119 as regards the Holy Father is punishable by reason of the law contained in canon 2343, § 1, joined with canon 2294, § 1.

CHAPTER VI

THE JURIDICAL DISPOSITION OF THE *DUBIUM FACTI* IN CANON 15

CANON 15 contains a twofold disposition of the matter concerning doubt in law. The first establishes the juridical principle that a *dubium iuris* deprives a law of its obligatory character. It now remains to consider the second aspect of the legislation relative to doubt. The determination set forth by the legislator as regards the *dubium facti* the writer proposes to study in two articles: in the one he will seek to explain the rule, and in the other he will endeavor to show the areas wherein the rule applies.

ARTICLE 1. THE MEANING OF THE RULE

The rule embodied in canon 15 regarding the doubt of fact reads as follows: however, in a doubt of fact the ordinary can dispense from them, provided they be laws from which the Roman Pontiff is wont to dispense.[1] At the very outset of this study, it is essential to note that the question of the *dubium facti* is placed in opposition to that of the *dubium iuris*. Indeed, the conjunction "*autem*" is adversative in character, and the construction of the canon seems to bear out the contention that, of its very nature, the doubt of fact will not remove the obligatory scope of a law. This is further borne out by the positive prescription that a dispensation is required.

The proper meaning of this rule is premised upon the correct appraisal of the several legal concepts which it encompasses. An exact analysis of this material will be attempted, and from this the sense of the legislation should become clear.

The fundamental notion to be clarified in this section of canon 15 is unquestionably that of the *dubium facti*. It would be false to assume that the concept of doubt as found in a doubt of fact

[1] *In dubio autem facti potest Ordinarius in eis dispensare, dummodo agatur de legibus in quibus Romanus Pontifex dispensare solet.*

substantially differs from that which is encountered in a doubt of law. In either instance, doubt is a state of mind in which a qualified assent is given to some proposition because of a positive and objective motive which is reasonably acceptable to a prudent man.[2] *Dubium iuris* and *dubium facti* differ in that their respective objects are specifically different. Indeed, it was previously shown that a doubt of law is intrinsically bound to the law itself, whether it concern its existence, its sense, its comprehension, or its cessation. Such a situation results in a norm which cannot be expected to guide certainly and clearly the conduct of men in a society.

A doubt of fact, as its name implies, is essentially centered on concrete facts, particular cases and circumstances. The existence of the law, as well as its signification and comprehension, are juridically indubitable. There is here no question of a vitiated legal norm; the law obtains as a perfect standard of human activity. The matter rests entirely on a particular case. It is uncertain that some fact or circumstance is governed by a law which certainly exists and whose sense and extent are definitely known.

A doubt of law, of its very nature, implies that a law was not adequately promulgated, or that it was poorly constructed. A doubt of fact, if assessed from the viewpoint of the law itself, suggests that the law is adequate, but that the relation of a particular fact to the existing law is not certain. A doubt of fact presupposes that the physical or juridical properties of a person or of a thing are such that it is difficult to ascertain whether or not the law applies to it. If, after study, it is discovered that the fact is definitely envisaged by the law, there cannot remain any doubt of fact. However, if it should remain uncertain that the fact is governed by an existing law, a doubt of fact has emerged. Canon 1250, for instance, adequately forbids the eating of meat and meat juices as the law of abstinence.[3] Yet, a doubt could arise whether a determined food must be classified

[2] Michiels, *Normae Generales*, I, 416. Cf. also the chapter where the concept of doubt is explored.

[3] *Abstinentiae lex vetat carne iureque ex carne vesci,...*

as meat. The obligation to abstain from meat is certain, but it is not certain that this food falls under the classification of meat. Hence, there exists a doubt of fact.

A doubt of fact emanates from the very nature of law itself. Law must needs be a general disposition. It is not possible for the legislator to foresee in all particulars the areas in which his enactment will obtain; and, granted that such could be the case, it would prove to be too cumbersome a task and it would inevitably result in confusion because of the prolixity which would attach to the legislation.[4] In short, universal law, however adequate it may be, must be limited to what is ordinary in human affairs and, as such, cannot provide for each and every circumstance and contingency. It is, then, a situation of this kind that provides the source of the various doubts of fact. Hence, a doubt of fact is any incertitude in which, for positive, objective and invincible motives, it cannot be certainly determined that a particular circumstance or condition really pertains to what is indubitably envisaged by a given law.

Canon 15 specifies that in a doubt of fact the ordinary can dispense from laws. The canonical concepts involved in this text will now be discussed. Canon 198, § 1, clearly states who in law is to be considered an ordinary. Ordinaries are, unless explicitly excepted, the Roman Pontiff, and for their respective territories, the residential bishop, abbot or prelate *nullius*, the vicar general, the apostolic administrator, the vicar apostolic, the prefect apostolic and those who, in default of any of these, temporarily succeed to the government either according to the provisions of the law or of approved constitutions; for their own subjects, the major superiors in exempt clerical religious institutes. These major superiors are the abbot primate, the abbot superior of a monastic congregation, the abbot of an independent monastery even though it belong to a monastic congregation, the superior general of a religious institute, the provincial superior, the vicars of all the afore-mentioned as well as those who have powers equivalent to the powers held by provincials.[5] It is also

[4] Suarez, *De Leg.*, Lib. VI, cap. VI, n. 4; cap. VII, n. 11.

[5] Canon 488, n. 8.

necessary to add that these major superiors must belong to an institute of either solemn or simple vows which has been withdrawn from the jurisdiction of the local ordinary [6] and to an institute the majority of whose members receive the Order of the priesthood.[7]

Ordinaries are all those who in accord with the norm of law have jurisdiction in the external forum. This jurisdiction is termed ordinary in the Code of Canon Law because it is attached to an office in the strict sense of the word [8] and because it is attached to that office by law.[9] This ordinary jurisdiction may be proper or vicarious.[10] It is proper if exercisable by one in his own name; it is vicarious if exercisable only in the name of another. A bishop, in the government of his own diocese, makes use of ordinary proper jurisdiction, but within that diocese, jurisdiction may also be exercised by a vicar general. Such a jurisdiction is ordinary because attached to the office by law,[11] but vicarious because it is exercisable only in the name of the bishop.

There is no special difficulty concerning the power which belongs to most ordinaries when they grant dispensations in the face of doubts of fact. However, because of the vicarious character of the ordinary power of the vicar general, it may be opportune to dwell briefly on the subject. The Code of Canon Law rules that the jurisdiction of the vicar general is coextensive with that of the bishop except in matters which the bishop has reserved to himself or which, according to law, require a special mandate of the bishop.[12] Thus, if a doubt of fact should arise relative to some matter which the bishop has reserved to himself, the vicar general would be unable to dispense from the law,

[6] Canon 488, n. 2.

[7] Canon 488, n. 4.

[8] Cf. canon 145.

[9] Canon 197, § 1.

[10] Canon 197, § 2.

[11] Canon 366, § 1.

[12] Canon 368, § 1.

and he could not, without a special mandate, grant a dispensation in the case of a doubt of fact with reference to which a special mandate is required for action by the vicar general.[13] It is abundantly clear that the vicar general in a doubt of fact may dispense if the matter has not been reserved to himself by the bishop, or if he has received a special mandate.

In the event that the see becomes vacant through the death of the bishop, all acts, except the conferring of benefices and ecclesiastical offices as accomplished by the vicar general before he received certain notice of the bishop's death, are valid; if the see becomes vacant through the resignation, transfer or removal of the bishop, all acts, except the conferring of benefices and offices, done by the vicar general up to the time when he learns that the Holy See has accepted the resignation, or has transferred or removed the bishop, are valid.[14] Thus, the granting of a dispensation in a doubt of fact would be a valid act in such circumstances according to the time when the favor is conceded.

The text of the law relative to the doubt of fact noted in canon 15 contains the words: "potest . . . dispensare," that is, the ordinary can dispense. Dispensation is defined as a relaxation of the law in a particular case.[15] However, it is a cardinal principle of the law concerning dispensations that a law can be relaxed only by the lawmaker, by his successor, by his superior, or by any person to whom any of these may have given the faculty.[16] This power of dispensing may be obtained either through a disposition of the law itself or in consequence of a particular concession of the proper authority. It is unquestionable that canon 15, when examined in the light of canon 81,[17]

[13] For a thorough analysis of the power of the vicar general acting with a special mandate, cf. Roelker, "The Vicar General and the Special Mandate," *The Jurist*, II (1942), 346-362.

[14] Canon 430, § 2.

[15] *Dispensatio, seu legis in casu speciali relaxatio* . . . Canon 80.

[16] Canon 80.

[17] *A generalibus Ecclesiae legibus Ordinarii infra Romanum Pontificem dispensare nequeunt, ne in casu quidem peculiari, nisi haec potestas eisdem fuerit explicite vel implicite concessa, aut nisi difficilis sit recursus ad*

contains an explicit juridical disposition by virtue of which an ordinary can dispense from a general law in the face of a doubt of fact. The limits which the legislator has established on this dispensatory power will be studied shortly.

Hence, it can be said that ordinaries, understood in the sense explained above, have received by law the right and competence of dispensing validly and licitly from a law when there exists a positive doubt of fact relative to the application of a law in a particular instance.[18] This power to dispense is premised on a true doubt of fact, so that the ordinary, upon verification of the factual doubt, can dispense inasmuch as the doubt of fact constitutes a just and reasonable cause for the concession of the dispensation.[19] The word "*potest*," however, does not necessarily imply that the ordinary is compelled to grant a dispensation, nor does it suggest that a subject has an inherent right to a dispensation. The ordinary must ever be mindful of his duty to examine a doubt of fact in order to determine if the doubt is such that there is need of a dispensation.

The laws which fall under this dispensatory power must now be examined. These are indicated in canon 15 by the words "*in eis*." It is indubitable that "*in eis*" must be referred to the previous proposition. Indeed, the legislator, as was shown earlier, specifically determined the effect of the *dubium iuris* on ecclesiastical laws. The legislation therein contained applied to all ecclesiastical laws; invalidating and disqualifying laws are explicitly adverted to for the sake of completeness. It follows that every species of ecclesiastical law can be the object of a dispensation in the face of a doubt of fact, provided that the law is one from which the Holy See is wont to dispense.

The last proposition of canon 15: "*dummodo agatur de legibus in quibus Romanus Pontifex dispensare solet*," sets up a limitation of the dispensatory power of ordinaries with respect to ecclesiastical laws. The crucial point in this matter rests on

---

Sanctam Sedem et simul in mora sit periculum gravis damni, et de dispensatione agatur quae a Sede Apostolica concedi solet.

18 Michiels, *Normae Generales*, I, 427-428.

19 Van Hove, *De Leg. Eccles.*, n. 231; Michiels, *Normae Generales*, I, 428.

the term "*solet.*" The Latin word can be identified with the English equivalents: it is usual, customary, wont or habitual. This connotes an ordinary mode or established practice of doing things and, as a result, necessarily rules out anything that would go beyond a regular pattern of action. Thus, anything that might exceed the usual and the customary could not be associated with the term "*solet.*"

The canonical authors, as a rule, do not examine this concept at any great length. Vermeersch-Creusen and Coronata, in their standard works, make no mention of it. Wernz-Vidal distinguish between dispensations which cannot be granted, or are never granted, or are not customarily granted, and dispensations which are more rarely, or more frequently, or regularly granted.[20] Others contrast the usual granting of a dispensation with the fact that some dispensations are never granted, or are rarely granted and then obtained only with difficulty.[21] Cicognani regards the style of the Roman Curia as the basis for what is to be considered ordinary and extraordinary in the line of granted dispensations.[22] Van Hove (1872-1947) was satisfied to point out that the Holy See never granted a dispensation in certain matters, while in others it does not habitually do so.[23] Gasparri (1852-1934) taught that matrimonial impediments of ecclesiastical origin do not all possess the same urgency in what concerns the attaining of the common good. Thus it is that a dispensation can never be obtained for certain impediments,

20 Wernz-Vidal, *Ius Canonicum,* T. V, *Ius Matrimoniale (3. ed., a P. Philippo Aguirre, S. I., recognita,* Romae: Apud Aedes Universitatis Gregorianae, 1946), n. 404, ad VI.

21 Rodrigo, *Praelectiones Theologico-Morales Comillenses,* Tom. II, *Tractatus de Legibus* (Santander: *Sal Terrae,* 1944), n. 466; *Traité de Droit Canonique* (publié sous la direction de Raoul Naz, 4 vols., Paris: Letouzey et Ané, 1946-1948), I, 218.

22 H. Cicognani-D. Staffa, *Commentarium ad Librum Primum Codicis Iuris Canonici* (2 vols., Romae: Ex Officina Typographica Romana "Buona Stampa", 1939-1942), II, 590.

23 Van Hove, *Commentarium Lovaniense in Codicem Iuris Canonici,* Tomus V, *De Privilegiis de Dispensationibus,* (Mechliniae-Romae: H. Dessain, 1939), n. 411.

rarely only for some other impediments, but even frequently from some others, sometimes only for a grave motive, but sometimes also for a lesser reason.[24]

The fact that a dispensation is rarely granted can originate in the relatively few requests for the dispensation as well as in the practice of the Roman Curia of denying the greater number of the petitions addressed to it. The standard of the rarity of concessions must be appraised in the light of that possible diversity. If a dispensation is rare because most requests for it are denied, then truly the dispensation is extraordinary and does not fall within the purview of the word "*solet*." On the other hand, the petitions for a particular dispensation may be relatively few, and yet habitually granted. In such an instance, there is nothing which goes beyond the scope of the regular and usual, and such a dispensation could readily be granted by an ordinary.

Consequently, the word "*solet*," as employed in canons 15 and 81, must be understood as contrasted with what never occurs or with what truly is exceptional. Thus, the dispensations contemplated in these canons are those which, in the normal course of affairs, are regularly granted by the Holy See whenever a cause proportionate to the law involved is verified. The dispensations which are not customarily granted are those which in ordinary adjuncts, even in the presence of a proportionate reason, are granted but exceptionally, that is, only in extraordinary circumstances, or only under unique conditions.[25] Such, for instance, was the dispensation granted by Pope Pius VII in 1801 to certain members of the clergy of France who had attempted marriage during the French Revolution. It is also noteworthy that Talleyrand (1754-1838), the former Bishop of Autun, never obtained a dispensation to relieve the diriment impediment of his episcopal Order.

At the present time, in the line of ecclesiastical impediments to marriage, only three impediments are excluded from the dispensatory power of ordinaries. Indeed, the Holy See is not wont

[24] Gasparri, *Tractatus Canonicus de Matrimonio* (2 vols., Romae: Typis Polyglottis Vaticanis, 1932), I, 169.

[25] Michiels, *Normae Generales*, II, 712.

to dispense from affinity in the direct line when the marriage has been consummated,[26] from the priesthood, and from solemn vows. All other impediments may be considered as offering customary matter for dispensation.

The sense of the rule contained in canon 15 may be briefly stated thus: when a positive and objective doubt arises whether a particular fact falls within the purview of a law which is certain and clear, all ordinaries can grant a relaxation from this law, provided that the dispensation is not one which is never or only exceptionally granted by the Holy See.

Article 2. The Principle Underlying This Rule

Before proceeding to the application of the rule concerning the *dubium facti,* one should perhaps indicate at least briefly the principle which underlies the positive enactment of the legislator. It is unmistakably clear that whenever a doubt of fact arises, the law itself is nowise directly affected. Indeed, the very notion of a doubt of fact is premised on the concept that the law is certain and clear in its existence, in its meaning, and in its comprehension. It follows, then, that in the presence of a doubt of fact the law necessarily retains its obligatory character. The juridical relation which exists between the subject and the law is adequately maintained. A doubt of fact does not impair this relation, for it implies, not a relation between a subject and the law, but a relation between a fact and the law itself quite independently of the subject. Indeed, the entire problem necessarily revolves around the judgment whether or not a particular fact is contemplated by the law.

It was to curb the anxieties which could arise regarding the lawfulness or the validity of acts performed under those circumstances that the legislator has set up in canon 15 a practical norm whose purpose it is to safeguard the lawfulness and the validity of acts in the face of a *dubium facti.* However, the mere presence of this enactment should not serve as an opportunity to deny the objective effects of the law, because the law remains a valid standard of human activity. The provision

[26] Canon 1043.

which has been here supplied by the legislator offers nothing that is strikingly new. The problem of doubt of fact was consistently studied by the theologians and the jurists, especially during the sixteenth and seventeenth centuries. It can be said that the Church has incorporated in its legislation the conclusion which emerged from their long controversies.

Before the advent of the Code of Canon Law, there existed two principal schools of thought relative to the disposition of a *dubium facti.* One, led by Suarez and St. Alphonsus, clung to the opinion that in the presence of a doubt of fact the safer course of action has to be followed.[27] This practical solution was premised on the consideration that the danger which is feared in the face of a doubt of fact is not affected in any way by one's appraisal of it. This peril is inherent in the fact itself.[28] Hence, there can be no sufficient excuse for acting, because, on the one hand, the law stands certain and clear as a norm of conduct, and thus one is under constraint to heed its obligatory force, and, on the other hand, there can exist as much likelihood that the fact falls within the purview of the law as there is possibility that it does not. As a consequence, because of the danger of running afoul of the law, there cannot be a sufficient excuse for acting.

However, while implicitly upholding the obligatory character of the law, Suarez did not construe his rule as an absolute standard. He duly recognized that in certain fields one could invoke other principles in order to obtain the necessary practical certitude. This was especially true with reference to penalties.[29]

The other school did not accept the distinction between a doubt of law and a doubt of fact as the primary basis of their solutions. Rather, they looked to the distinction between what was licit and what had necessarily to be done for the achieving of a particular end. As a result, in a doubt of fact concerning the lawfulness of an act, they held the view that there was no

[27] Suarez, *De Bon. et Mal. Act. Hum.*, Disp. XII, sect. VI, nn. 8-10; St. Alphonsus, *Theologia Moralis*, Lib. I, n. 41 ss., n. 63, n. 77.

[28] Suarez, *De Bon. et Mal. Act. Hum.*, Disp. XII, sect. VI, n. 10.

[29] Suarez, *De Bon. et Mal. Act. Hum.*, Disp. XII, sect. V, n. 8.

compulsion to forestall the possible peril which might arise from one's actions, so long as a moral obligation did not arise from another quarter, such as the precepts of justice, charity and religion. In respect of the validity of an act, they held the same view as Suarez and St. Alphonsus: *in dubiis tutior pars est sequenda.*[30] The proponents of the latter opinion were primarily theologians. They were principally concerned with morality, and the legal field offered little of interest to them, save for the evident moral implications inherent in law. Suarez, on the other hand, combined a great talent for theology with a wide knowledge of the philosophy of law. He possessed a great reverence for matters legal, and this resulted in his stand that, so long as a law is duly constituted and promulgated, the obligation flowing therefrom must be respected and upheld.

In the writer's opinion, the position of Suarez is more consonant with the principles of jurisprudence, and it reflects more validly the mind of the legislator. The mere fact that an ordinary can grant a dispensation in the face of a doubt of fact necessarily postulates that the legislator expected his law to be binding. The dispensation is provided for the purpose of assuring the lawfulness or the validity of an act when it is doubtful that the act is within the purview of the law. If one were to act without a relaxation of the law, one would be doing so at one's own risk.[31] Ignorance or a probable opinion does not transform a doubtful fact into a certain fact; this is always extrinsic to the agent. The very disposition of the law as it regards the doubt of fact presupposes that the legislator desired that his subjects make use of the positive remedies provided by law to insure the lawfulness and validity of their acts; otherwise he would have needlessly legislated.

It was shown earlier that Suarez contemplated the possibility that the obligation of a law may cease in some particular in-

[30] Vasquez, *Commentariorum ac Disputationum in Primam Secundae Sancti Thomae Tomus Secundus* (ed. novissima, 2 vols., Lugduni, 1631), Disp. 63, cap. 1; Disp. 65, cap. 3; Disp. 67, cap. 2; Laymann, *Theologia Moralis in Quinque Libros Distributa* (2 vols., Venetiis, 1630), Lib. I, Tract. I, cap. 5, §§ 3 and 4.

[31] Wernz-Vidal, *Normae Generales*, p. 245.

stance even if the legislator has not removed the over-all obligatory character of the law.[32] While law is a universal disposition, it must be limited to what is ordinary in human affairs. It would be impractical to expect a legislator to foresee all the circumstances and contingencies to which his law will be subjected. Hence, in some particular instance the obligation of law will cease, not because the legal enactment is abrogated, but because the legislator cannot reasonably urge it. However, it would be perilous to invoke too frequently this particular situation, since of its very nature law is conceived as a provision for the common good, and as such will necessarily embrace the great majority of cases. A solid knowledge of the law along with a judicious exercise of prudence is a prime requisite in this particular field.

Various authors, commenting on canon 15 of the Code of Canon Law, have offered practical solutions to this problem. Van Hove[33] held that, when the doubt of fact bears solely on the lawfulness of an act, there is no necessity of seeking a dispensation, although it might perhaps be more fitting to encourage the request for one. In the case wherein validity is at stake, he insisted that a dispensation be obtained beforehand. Ojetti (1862-1932)[34] and Vermeersch (1858-1936)-Creusen[35] upheld the view that the law obliges at all times, even when lawfulness alone is involved. However, they made an exception to this broad statement to provide for the possible conversion of a doubt of fact into a doubt of law in certain cases when only lawfulness is encountered. Thus they required that a dispensation be sought as a normal course. Rodrigo maintains that a doubt of fact does not detract from the objective obligation of the law.[36] Yet he holds that beyond the case of invalidating laws

[32] Cf. *supra,* p. 42.

[33] *De Leg. Eccles.*, n. 231.

[34] *Commentarium in Codicem Iuris Canonici* (4 vols., Romae: Apud Aedes Universitatis Gregorianae, 1927-1931), Lib. I, *Normae Generales,* p. 126.

[35] *Epitome Iuris Canonici* (3 vols., Romae-Mechliniae: H. Dessain), Tomus I (7. ed., 1949), n. 113.

[36] *Tractatus de Legibus,* n. 417.

a dispensation is not necessary, save for the purpose of staving off in the external forum the juridical effect of presumed crime.[37]

The considerations offered by these and other authors in some form or other indicate a preponderance of opinion relative to the objective obligatory character of the law in the case of a doubt of fact.[38] The various practical solutions which are proposed vary according to the diversified adherence shown to the pre-Code schools of thought on the subject. Thus, a greater or a lesser stress for the need of a dispensation constitutes the invariable pattern consistent with the philosophy of law which is embraced.

Article 3. Specific Application of the Rule

After a rather lengthy study of the principle underlying the rule enacted by the legislator in canon 15 for the treatment of a doubt of fact, it now remains to consider the relation of the *dubium facti* with the various species of laws. The principle which must ever be honored in the course of this article is the following: notwithstanding the doubt of fact, the law still binds. It is assumed that the law has been properly constituted and duly promulgated, so that it is a valid norm for human activity. All of this explains and justifies the distinction which has been established between a doubt of law and a doubt of fact in canon 15, as Michiels so aptly expresses it.[39]

a. Preceptive and Prohibitory Laws

It was shown earlier that the sole efficacy of preceptive and prohibitory laws resides in the obligation which they induce.[40] These laws exclusively mean to indicate in a positive or in a

[37] *Tractatus de Legibus*, n. 423.

[38] Cf. Cicognani-Staffa, *Commentarium ad Librum Primum Codicis Iuris Canonici*, I, 240; II, 109; Maroto, *Institutiones Iuris Canonici ad Normam Novi Codicis*, Tomus I (3. ed., Romae: Apud Commentarium pro Religiosis, 1921), n. 230, ad 2; Michiels, *Normae Generales*, I, 430-432.

[39] *Normae Generales*, I, p. 431, footnote 2.

[40] Cf. *supra*, p. 63.

negative manner what is lawful and what is unlawful. So long as these laws are properly constituted and promulgated, they conserve their obligatory character at all times, unless they be abrogated. Thus, they do not lose this characteristic in the face of a doubt of fact. However, when a doubt of fact does arise, the subject of the law knows the law and its obligation, and yet there is a positive and objective doubt in his mind as to whether or not the case in question is envisioned by the law. What is he to do? Two courses are open to him: either he will seek a dispensation from the law and assure the lawfulness of his act, or he will attempt to go along on the assumption that this particular situation was not foreseen by the legislator, and consequently does not fall within the purview of the law.[41] The first course is surely the safer of the two, since the legislator has positively provided for this eventuality in canon 15. The second course offers a danger in that, if a penalty lurks for the external violation of the preceptive or prohibitory law, the subject could be brought to task for this presumed infraction of the law. It is true that in such a situation no moral guilt and, as will be shown later, no penalty are incurred, because these presuppose that the subject knew his obligation and voluntarily acted contrary to it: such is clearly not the case here. It is then more consonant with the legislation of canon 15, and thus also more prudent, to seek a dispensation in such instances. In practice, however, it may prove difficult to have recourse to the ordinary, for oftentimes a quick solution will be necessary.

The following are offered as examples of a doubt of fact in the face of preceptive and prohibitory laws. Canon 1248 prescribes that on feast days of obligation Mass must be heard.[42] It can readily occur that a subject, while fully aware of the law, may find himself in such particular circumstances that he will doubt whether a given day is a feast day of obligation or not. If due efforts at dispelling the doubt prove futile, the doubt is a true doubt of fact. The same canon also prescribes that one

[41] Cf. *supra*, p. 88.

[42] *Festis de praecepto diebus Missa audienda est . . .*

may not engage in servile works on feast days of obligation.[43] Theological doctrine and customary practice largely determine what constitutes servile work. Yet, there may emerge a type of activity regarding which there is no accepted certainty that it falls within the category of servile works. If, after due investigation, it cannot be certainly determined that this activity constitutes servile work, a doubt of fact has arisen.

The law of abstinence forbids taking as nourishment meat and meat juices.[44] The Code of Canon Law does not define flesh meat; this is left to the common human appraisal and custom. However, a case may readily arise when one, while fully cognizant of the law, will doubt whether or not a determined food is included in the accepted category of meat. He is then laboring under a doubt of fact.

b. INVALIDATING AND DISQUALIFYING LAWS

An invalidating law is, in a broad sense, any law that declares an act invalid if it be performed contrary to the tenor of the law. It can consider the person performing the act or the act itself. In both instances, the legal effect of the act is denied quite independently of physical capacity or of good or bad faith. Invalidating laws, as distinguished from preceptive or prohibitory laws, in the majority of cases produce two effects: invalidity and obligation. When the legislator enacts an invalidating law, he must necessarily intend that invalidity will brand the act that is done contrary to his law. However, some invalidating laws immediately produce their effects in both the internal and the external forum, while others require a judicial sentence, so that the acts performed in contravention of such invalidating laws are presumed valid until the sentence is pronounced.

The validity of an act is not in the least affected by one's appraisal of it. The act is valid only if it matches the legal stand-

[43] ... *et abstinendum ab operibus servilibus, actibus forensibus, itemque, nisi aliud ferant legitimae consuetudines aut peculiaria indulta, publico mercatu, nundinis, aliisque publicis emptionibus et venditionibus.*

[44] Canon 1250.

ard established by the legislator. In a doubt of fact, an invalidating law does not lose its efficacy, since the law is certain and clear, and the doubt is centered simply on a particular fact in relation to a given law. Thus, ecclesiastical law prescribes for the validity of a marriage that a man have completed his sixteenth year, and a woman her fourteenth year.[45] However, in some particular contingency it may prove impossible to determine whether or not one of the parties has reached the canonical age: this is a doubt of fact. A dispensation "*ad cautelam*" should be obtained in assurance of the validity of the marriage. It matters not that, if the union be contracted without the necessary dispensation, it enjoys for its presumptive validity the full favor of law.[46] Indeed, should the subsequently obtained certain knowledge of the age of one of the consorts reveal a deficiency in the age set up as requisite in the invalidating law, the marriage would have to be judged invalid. The obtaining of a dispensation is the only effective manner of forestalling the risk of invalidity when a doubt of fact is at hand.

C. PENAL LAWS

Penal law is that which decrees a penalty. In ecclesiastical legislation, a penalty is defined as the privation of some good invoked for the correction of the culprit and for the punishment of a crime, and inflicted by the legitimate authority.[47] A penalty thus presupposes an external and morally imputable violation of a law to which some canonical sanction is attached.[48] Moral imputability postulates that the law be known and that it be willfully violated. A doubt of fact, of its very nature, arises when it is positively and objectively doubtful whether some particular contingency is envisaged by the law. In the case of a doubt of fact, it must be emphatically stated that the penal law itself is not the object of the doubt. The law is certain and clear

[45] Canon 1067, § 1.

[46] Canon 1014.

[47] Canon 2215.

[48] Canon 2195, § 1.

in its existence, its meaning and its extent. If such were not the case, then a *dubium iuris* would be had and the law would not oblige. The precise point at issue is to determine if the external violation of a penal law is morally imputable when a doubt of fact is present. If a particular fact were certainly and clearly punishable by the law, there would be no doubt of fact, and the subject who, notwithstanding the enacted punishment, would nonetheless act, would incur the penalty enjoined by the law. But in this case there is present a positive and an objective doubt whether or not this particular fact falls within the purview of the penal law. The external violation of the law and the consequent moral imputability are necessarily doubtful, and the subject will not be conscious of having committed a delict. He has not then incurred a *latae sententiae* penalty.[49] Nor would he incur a *ferendae sententiae* penalty, for the law provides that no penalty can be inflicted unless it be certain that a crime has been committed.[50]

Thus, for the infliction of a penalty, it must be certain that all the elements postulated for a canonical delict are present, and this can be obtained only from complete and evident proof that a crime was committed.

d. IMPEDIMENTS AND DOUBT OF FACT

It would be false to assume that the legislation as enacted in canon 15 concerning the doubt of fact is the ultimate legal standard for all doubts of fact. The legislator has, in a number of instances, established very definite lines of conduct which must be closely followed in certain matters. The principal area of this departure is found in the impediments to marriage. Ecclesiastical law, echoing the prohibitions of the natural law, forbids marriage between persons who are related in the direct line of consanguinity or in the first degree of the collateral line. If within these limits there arise a doubt regarding the relationship of persons wishing to intermarry, and the doubt should prove insoluble, this is a doubt of fact. Under such circumstances,

[49] Canon 2232, § 1.

[50] Canon 2233, § 1.

canon 1076, § 3, decrees that such a marriage is never permitted.[51]

The same holds true relative to a prior union. It is forbidden to contract another marriage, even if the first is invalid or has been dissolved, before the nullity of the first or its dissolution is legitimately and certainly proved.[52] Indeed, before proof is adduced, a doubt of fact exists relative to the validity of the first marriage. This doubt of fact stands in the face either of the natural or the positive divine law. The human legislator cannot grant a dispensation, since for the relaxing of such a law he has no competence. Thus, the doubt of fact must effectively and certainly be solved before a second marriage may be contracted.

Impotence, antecedent and perpetual, invalidates marriage in consequence of the law of nature itself.[53] It is certainly possible that one who contemplates the contracting of marriage may have a solid doubt regarding his freedom from impotence. This is a doubt of fact. Yet, the prescription of the Code of Canon Law does not advert to canon 15, but simply decrees that the marriage is not to be hindered.[54] This is another departure from the ordinary treatment of the doubt of fact.

Canon 1014 presents the favor of law which a marriage enjoys in the face of a doubt.[55] The legislator has prescribed the consistent maintaining of this presumption. It must be overridden with irrefutable proof before a marriage will be declared null and void. This is a far cry from the legislation of canon 15. Canon 1070, § 2, provides that when the baptism of a party was doubtful, the marriage must be regarded as valid according

[51] *Nunquam matrimonium permittatur, si quod subsit dubium num partes sint consanguineae in aliquo gradu lineae rectae aut in primo gradu lineae collateralis.*

[52] Canon 1069, § 2.

[51] Canon 1068, § 1.

[53] Canon 1068, § 2. *Si impedimentum impotentiae dubium sit, sive dubio iuris sive dubio facti, matrimonium non est impediendum.*

[55] *Matrimonium gaudet favore iuris; quare in dubio standum est pro valore matrimonii, donec contrarium probetur, salvo praescripto can. 1127.*

to canon 1014, until it is certainly established that one of the parties was certainly baptized and the other was not. Thus a doubt of fact would not suffice to invalidate a marriage.

Then, too, in a doubt of fact, the privilege of the faith enjoys the favor of law.[56] This doubt does not change the objective fact which is in question, but it serves to legitimize the new marriage, and it permits the dissolution of an earlier one even if it is valid. The doubt of fact, in such a contingency, takes on an importance which canon 15 does not foresee.

[56] Canon 1127.

CONCLUSIONS

The following conclusions are offered as a result of this study:

1. The doctrine, as found in the *Corpus Iuris Canonici* and the Decretalists, is definitely not an organic and systematic treatment of doubt in law. Yet, it contains the elements which led to the elaboration of the present legislation.
2. In the medieval solution of cases affected with doubt, tutiorism, despite a few exceptional instances, prevailed. However, it did not hold sway in the penal field, wherein the criminal fact needed to be established with definite proof before punishment could be meted out.
3. While the medieval jurists postulated clarity as an element in law, and acknowledged for a doubtful law nothing more than a minimum of obligation, they did not hold that a doubtful law, as such, was destitute of all obligatory character.
4. The doubt of law and the doubt of fact, as envisaged in canon 15, must be understood to refer solely to ecclesiastical laws and their implied obligations.
5. The concept of a *dubium iuris* touches not only the existence, the sense and the comprehension of an ecclesiastical law, but also the permanence of such a law.
6. With reference to an invalidating or a penal law, it is always essential to determine whether the doubt of law affects the entire structure of the law, or whether it simply relates to a component part of the law. In the latter event, the area which is clearly not doubtful retains its efficacy.
7. The legislation concerning the doubt of fact is based on the principle that the law is a true legal norm, and as such carries obligatory force. Hence, it follows that to insure certainly the lawfulness, and possibly also the validity of the acts, a dispensation should be sought in such instances.

BIBLIOGRAPHY

Sources

Acta Apostolicae Sedis, Commentarium Officiale, Romae, 1909-1929; Civitate Vaticana, 1929-

Bouscaren, T. Lincoln, *The Canon Law Digest*, 2 vols. and Supplement through 1948, Milwaukee, Wis.: The Bruce Publishing Co., 1934-1943-1949.

Codex Iuris Canonici Pii X Pontificis Maximi iussu digestus, Benedicti Papae XV auctoritate promulgatus, Praefatione, Fontium Annotatione et Indice Analytico-Alphabetico ab Emo Petro Card. Gasparri Auctus, Romae: Typis Polyglottis Vaticanis, 1917; reimpressio, Civitate Vaticana, 1933.

Codicis Iuris Canonici Fontes, cura Emi Petri Card. Gasparri editi, 9 vols., Romae (postea Civitate Vaticana): Typis Polyglottis Vaticanis, 1923-1939. (Vols. VII-IX, ed. cura et studio Emi Iustiniani Card. Serédi).

Corpus Iuris Canonici, ed. Lipsiensis secunda, post Aemilii Ludovici Richter curas . . . instruxit Aemilius Friedberg, 2 vols., Lipsiae, 1879-1881.

Corpus Iuris Civilis, 3 vols., Berolini, 1928-1929. Vol. I, ed. stereotypa 15., *Institutiones*, quae recognovit P. Krueger; Vol. I, ed. stereotypa 15., *Digesta*, quae recognovit T. Mommsen et retractavit P. Krueger; Vol. II, ed. stereotypa 10., *Codex Iustinianus*, quem recognovit et retractavit P. Krueger; Vol. III, ed. stereotypa 5., *Novellae*, quas recognovit R. Schoell et absolvit G. Kroll.

Decretales D. Gregorii Papae IX, suae integritati una cum glossis restitutae, cum privilegio Gregorii XIII, Pont. Max., et Aliorum Principum, Romae, 1582.

Decretum Gratiani emendatum et notationibus illustratum una cum glossis, Gregorii XIII, Pont. Max., iussu editum, 2 vols., Romae, 1582.

Denzinger, Henricus-Bannwart, Clemens et Umberg, Iohannes Baptista, *Enchiridion Symbolorum, Definitionum et Declarationum de Rebus Fidei et Morum*, ed. 26 augment., Friburgi Brisgoviae: Herder, 1947.

Hinschius, Paulus, *Decretales Pseudo-Isidorianae et Capitula Angilramni*, Lipsiae, 1863.

Jaffé, Philippus, *Regesta Pontificum Romanorum ab condita Ecclesia ad annum post Christum natum MCXCVIII*, ed. 2 correctam et auctam auspiciis Guglielmi Wattenbach curaverunt F. Kaltenbrunner, P. Ewald, S. Loewenfeld, 2 vols., Lipsiae, 1885-1888.

Liber Sextus Decretalium D. Bonifacii Papae VIII, suae integritati una cum Clementinis et Extravagantibus, earumque Glossis restitutis, Romae, 1582.

Potthast, Augustus, *Regesta Pontificum Romanorum inde ab anno post Christum natum MCXCVIII ad annum MCCCIV*, 2 vols., Berolini, 1874-1875.

Reference Works

Alphonsus M. de Ligorio, St., *Theologia Moralis*, 4 vols., cujus editionem criticam curavit L. Gaudé, Romae: Typographia Polyglotta Vaticana, 1905-1912.

Blat, Albertus, *Commentarium Textus Codicis Iuris Canonici*, 6 vols., Romae: Ex Typographia Pontificia in Instituto Pii IX, 1919-1927.

Brys, Joseph, *Juris Canonici Compendium*, 10. ed., 2 vols., Brugis: Desclée de Brouwer et Socii, 1947-1949.

Cappello, Felix, *Tractatus Canonico-Moralis de Sacramentis*, 5 vols., Vol. V, 6. ed., Taurini-Romae: Marietti, 1950.

———, *Summa Iuris Canonici*, 3 vols., Vol. I, 4. ed., Romae: Apud Aedes Universitatis Gregorianae, 1945.

———, *Tractatus Canonico-Moralis de Censuris*, 4. ed., Taurini-Romae: Marietti, 1950.

Chelodi, I.-Ciprotti, P., *Ius Canonicum de Matrimonio*, 5. ed., Vicenza: Società Anonima, 1947.

Cicognani, Hamletus I.-Staffa, D., *Commentarium ad Librum Primum Codicis Iuris Canonici*, Romae: Ex Officina Typographica Romana "Buona Stampa", 1939-1942.

Cicognani, Amleto Giovanni, *Canon Law*, 2. ed., revised, authorized English version by O'Hara and Brennan, Philadelphia: The Dolphin Press, 1935, reprinted Westminster, Md.: The Newman Press, 1949.

Claeys-Bouuaert, F., et Simenon, G., *Manuale Juris Canonici*, 3 vols., Vol. I, 3. ed., Gandae et Leodii: Dessain, 1947.

Coronata, Matthaeus Conte a, *Institutiones Iuris Canonici*, 2. ed., 5 vols., Taurini: Marietti, 1939-1947.

D'Annibale, Josephus, *Summula Theologiae Moralis*, 5. ed., 3 vols., Romae, 1908.

De Ghellinck, Joseph, *Le Mouvement Théologique du XIIe siècle*, 2. ed., Bruges: Editions "de Tempel", Bruxelles: L'Edition Universelle, Paris: Desclée de Brouwer, 1948.

De Mauri, L., *Regulae Juris*, 11. ed., Milano: Hoepli, 1949.

Dictionnaire de Droit Canonique, commencé sous la direction de A. Villien et E. Magnin (1924), continué sous la direction de A. Amanieu (1926), publié sous la direction de Raoul Naz (1934), Paris: Letouzey et Ané, 1935–

Dictionnaire de Théologie Catholique, 16 vols. in 32, Paris: Letouzey et Ané, 1903-1952.

Fagnanus, Prosper, *Commentarium in Quinque Libros Decretalium*, 5 vols. in 4, Venetiis, 1696-1697.

Gasparri, P., *Tractatus Canonicus de Matrimonio*, ed. nova ad mentem Codicis Iuris Canonici, 2 vols., Civitati Vaticanae: Typis Polyglottis Vaticanis, 1932.

Gury, Joannes, *Compendium Theologiae Moralis*, 2. ed., 2 vols., Romae, 1869.

Hostiensis, Cardinalis (Henricus de Segusio), *Commentaria in Quinque Decretalium Libros*, 5 vols., Venetiis, 1581.

Ioannes Andreae, *In Quinque Decretalium Libros Novella Commentaria*, 5 vols., Venetiis, 1581.

Jone, Heribertus, *Commentarium in Codicem Iuris Canonici*, Vol. I, Paderborn: Officina Libraria F. Schöningh, 1950.

Laymann, P., *Theologia Moralis in Quinque Libros Distributa*, ed. nova ab auctore recognita et primum in Italia excusa, 2 vols., Venetiis, 1630.

Lohmuller, Martin, *The Promulgation of Law*, The Catholic University of America Canon Law Studies, n. 241, Washington, D. C.: The Catholic University of America Press, 1947.

Lottin, Dom Odon, *Psychologie et Morale aux XIIe et XIIIe Siècles*, 3 tomes in 4 vols., Louvain: Abbaye du Mont-César, et Gembloux: J. Duculot, 1942-1949.

Maroto, Ph., *Institutiones Iuris Canonici*, 2 vols., Romae, 1919-1921. Vol. I, 3. ed., 1921.

Michiels, Gommarus, *Normae Generales Iuris Canonici*, 2. ed., 2 vols., Parisiis-Tornaci-Romae: Desclée et Socii, 1949.

Ojetti, B., *Commentarium in Codicem Iuris Canonici*, 4 vols., Romae: Apud Aedes Universitatis Gregorianae, 1927-1931.

Ottaviani, Alaphridus, *Institutiones Iuris Publici Ecclesiastici*, 2 vols., Vol. I, 3. ed., Civitati Vaticanae: Typis Polyglottis Vaticanis, 1947.

Panormitanus, Abbas (Nicolaus de Tudeschis), *Commentaria in Quinque Libros Decretalium*, 5 vols. in 7, Venetiis, 1588.

Philippot, Robertus, *De Dubio in Iure praesertim Canonico*, Brugis: Editiones Caroli Beyaert, 1947.

Pirhing, Ernricus, *Ius Canonicum in Quinque Libros Decretalium*, 5 vols. in 4, Dilingae, 1722.

Reiffenstuel, Anacletus, *Ius Canonicum Universum*, 5 vols. in 7, Parisiis: L. Vivès, 1864-1870.

Roberti, Francesco, *De Delictis et Poenis*, Vol. I, pars 1a et 2a, Romae: Libraria Pontificii Instituti Utriusque Iuris, 1938.

Rodrigo, Lucius, *Praelectiones Theologico-Morales Comillenses*, Tomus II, *Tractatus de Legibus*, Santander: Editorialis Sal Terrae, 1944.

Schmalzgrueber, Franciscus, *Ius Ecclesiasticum Universum*, 5 vols. in 12, Romae, 1843-1845.

Schmidt, John Rogg, *The Principles of Authentic Interpretation in Canon 17 of the Code of Canon Law*, The Catholic University of America Canon Law Studies, n. 141, Washington, D. C.: The Catholic University of America Press, 1941.

Suarez, Franciscus, *Opera Omnia*, 26 vols., Parisiis: L. Vivès, 1856-1866. Vol. IV, *Tractatus de Bonitate et Malitia Actuum Humanorum*, 1856; Vols. V & VI, *Tractatus de Legibus et Legislatore Deo*, 1856.

Thomas, Alphonsus J., *The Juridical Effect of Doubtful Cessation of Law According to the Code of Canon Law*, Les Thèses Canoniques de Laval, n. 9, Québec: Faculté de Droit Canonique, Université Laval, 1949.

Thomas Aquinas, St., *Opera Omnia*, iussu impensaque Leonis XIII, Pontificis Maximi edita, Romae: Typographia polyglotta Sacrae Congregationis de Propaganda Fide, 1882-19—. *Summa Theologiae*, Vols. IV-XI, 1889-1903.

———, *Quaestiones Disputatae*, Vol. I, *De Veritate*, cura et studio P. Fr. Raymundi Spiazzi, O.P., 8. ed. revisa, Taurini-Romae: Marietti, 1949.

Traité de Droit Canonique, publié sous la direction de Raoul Naz, 4 vols., Paris: Letouzey et Ané, 1947-1949.

Van Hove, A., *Commentarium Lovaniense in Codicem Iuris Canonici*, 1 vol. in 5 tomes, Tom. I, *Prolegomena*, 2. ed., Mechliniae-Romae: H. Dessain, 1945; Tom. II, *De Legibus Ecclesiasticis*, Mechliniae-Romae: H. Dessain, 1930; Tom. IV, *De Rescriptis*, Mechliniae-Romae H. Dessain, 1936; Tom. V, *De Privilegiis-De Dispensationibus*, Mechliniae-Romae: H. Dessain, 1939.

Vasquez, G., *Commentariorum ac Disputationum in Primam Secundae Sancti Thomae Tomus Secundus*, ed. novissima, 2 vols., Lugduni, 1631.

Vermeersch, A.-Creusen, J., *Epitome Iuris Canonici*, 3 vols., Vol. I, 7. ed., 1949; Vol. II, 6. ed., 1940; Vol. III, 6. ed., 1946, Mechlinae-Romae: H. Dessain.

Vlaming, T.-Bender, L., *Praelectiones Iuris Matrimonii*, 4. ed., Bussum in Hollandia: Paulus Brand, 1950.

Waffelaert, G., *De Dubio Solvendo in Re Morali*, Lovanii, 1880.

Wernz, Franciscus-Vidal, Petrus, *Ius Canonicum ad Codicis Normam Exactum*, 7 vols. in 8, Vol. I, 2. ed., 1952; Vol. II, 3. ed. a P. Aguirre recognita, 1943; Vol. III, 1933; Vol. IV, pars 1, 1934; pars 2, 1935; Vol. V, 3. ed. a P. Aguirre recognita, 1946; Vol. VI, 2. ed. a F. Cappello recognita, 1949; Vol. VII, 2. ed., 1951, Romae: Apud Aedes Universitatis Gregorianae.

Articles

Brisbois, E., "Pour le probabilisme," *Ephemerides Theologicae Lovanienses*, XIII (1936), 74-97.

Chollet, A., "Doute," *Dictionnaire de Théologie Catholique*, Tome IV, 2e partie (1939), 1811-1820.

Damen, C., "De vitanda iuris correctione ad normam Codicis," *Apollinaris*, V (1932), 54-68; 199-209.

Deman, T., "Probabilisme," *Dictionnaire de Théologie Catholique*, Tome XIII, 1ère partie (1936), 417-619.

Lopez, U., "Thesis Probabilismi ex Sancto Thoma demonstrata," *Periodica de Re Morali, Canonica, Liturgica*, XXV (1936), 38-49; XXVI (1937), 17-33.

Naz, R., "Doute," *Dictionnaire de Droit Canonique*, Tome IV (1949), 1437-1445.

Ranwez, E., "A propos du probabilisme," *Nouvelle Revue Théologique*, LVI (1929), 552-564.

Roelker, Edward, "The Concept of Invalidating Laws," *The Jurist*, III (1943), 32-63.

———, "The Power to Enact Invalidating Laws," *The Jurist*, III (1943), 231-257.

———, "The Interpretation of Invalidating Laws," *The Jurist*, III (1943), 364-403.

———, "The Effect and Obligation of Invalidating Laws," *The Jurist*, III (1943), 550-566.

———, "The Vicar General and the Special Mandate," *The Jurist*, II (1942), 346-362.

Periodicals

Apollinaris, Romae, 1928–

Ephemerides Theologicae Lovanienses, Louvain, 1924–

Jurist, The, Washington, D. C., 1941–

Nouvelle Revue Théologique, Paris, 1869–

Periodica de Religiosis et Missionariis, Brugis, 1905-1919; from 1920: *Periodica de Re Canonica et Morali, utilia praesertim Religiosis et Missionariis*, Brugis, 1920-1927; *Periodica de Re Morali, Canonica, Liturgica*, Brugis, 1927-1936, et Romae, 1937–

Abbreviations

C.—*Codex Iustinianus* or Causa

c.—Canon or caput

D.—*Digestum Iustinianum* or Distinctio

J E—Jaffé, *Regesta Pontificum Romanorum* (edited by P. Ewald; for the years 590-882).

J K—Jaffé, *op. cit.* (edited by F. Kaltenbrunner; to the year 590).

J L—Jaffé, *op. cit.* (edited by S. Loewenfeld; for the years 882-1198).

BIOGRAPHICAL NOTE

Roger Viau was born August 10, 1916, in Holyoke, Massachusetts, and there attended the School of the Precious Blood. He received his secondary education at Assumption College, Worcester, Massachusetts. After a two-year stay at the Seminary of Philosophy, Montreal, Canada, he pursued his theological studies at the School of Theology, Laval University, Quebec, Canada, where he obtained the Licentiate in Sacred Theology. He was ordained to the priesthood on June 19, 1943, in Springfield, Massachusetts. He served for seven years as assistant at the Church of the Precious Blood, Holyoke, Massachusetts. In September, 1950, he entered the School of Canon Law at The Catholic University of America, Washington, D. C. He received the Baccalaureate in Canon Law in June, 1951, and the Licentiate in Canon Law in June, 1952.

ALPHABETICAL INDEX

CANON LAW STUDIES *

337. Bourque, Rev. John R., S.T.L., J.C.L., The judicial power of the Church—Canon 1553, § 1.
338. Cornell, Rev. Charles E., A.B., S.T.B., J.C.L., The juridical status of heretics and schismatics in good faith.
339. Fitzgerald, Rev. William Francis, A.B., S.T.L., J.C.L., The parish census and the *liber status animarum*.
340. Kubik, Rev. Stanislaus J., S.T.D., J.C.L., Invalidity of dispensations according to canon 84, § 1.
341. Nugent, Rev. John Gerard, C.M., J.C.L., Ordination in societies of the common life.
342. Peterson, Rev. Casimir Melvyn, S.S., A.B., S.T.L., J.C.L., Spiritual care in diocesan seminaries.
343. Reiss, Rev. John Charles, A.B., S.T.L., J.C.L., The time and place of sacred ordination.
344. Sheehan, Rev. Joseph George, J.C.L., The obligation of respect and obedience of clerics to their ordinary.
345. Shekleton, Rev. Matthew M., O.S.M., J.C.L., Doctrinal interpretation of law.
346. Viau, Rev. Roger, S.T.L., J.C.L., Doubt in Canon Law.
347. Walsh, Rev. Donnell A., A.B., J.C.L., The new law on secular institutes.
348. Sesto, Rev. Gennaro Joseph, S.D.B., A.B., S.T.L., J.C.L., Guardians of the mentally ill in ecclesiastical trials.
349. Fus, Rev. Edward A., A.B., J.C.L., The extraordinary form of marriage according to canon 1098.

* For a complete list of the available numbers of this series apply to the Catholic University of America Press, 620 Michigan Avenue, N.E., Washington (17), D. C.

www.ingramcontent.com/pod-product-compliance
Lightning Source LLC
LaVergne TN
LVHW050204080826
844660LV00012B/348

* 9 7 8 0 8 1 3 2 2 5 1 4 2 *